GAINING LIGHTNESS

WEIGHT MANAGEMENT THROUGH SELF DISCOVERY

BY BOB WOLFE

WITH PATSY SYKES

Printed in the United States of America.

ISBN 10: 1-59571-221-6
ISBN 13: 978-1-59571-221-9

Library of Congress Control Number: 2008920779

Word Association Publishers
205 Fifth Avenue
Tarentum, Pennsylvania 15084

www.wordassociation.com
1.800.827.7903

Book Design: Gina Datres, Word Association Publishers

TIP THE SCALES IN YOUR FAVOR

SPIRIT

MIND

BODY

GAINING
LIGHTNESS

WEIGHT MANAGEMENT
THROUGH SELF DISCOVERY

TABLE OF CONTENTS

TABLE OF CONTENTS CONT'D.

DEDICATION

This book is dedicated to my Mother, Doris Louise Wolfe who struggled with weight management for most of her life. Since my teen years, she inspired my writing pursuits; and her quest to lose weight (gain lightness) inspired me to develop this program so that others experiencing her difficulties with success would have the resources to meet their goals. And, to my Father, DuBree Arlo Wolfe who was (at least in my mind) the master of moderation and always encouraged everyone he met to follow their path, wherever it may lead them. God rest their souls as they have attained the ultimate in Gaining Lightness.

ACKNOWLEDGEMENTS

I would like to acknowledge and lovingly thank my wife, Cindy who has always encouraged my endeavors with her belief in me. I would also like to thank my hypnotherapy teachers, Dr. Allen Chips and Dr. William Horton; and especially Lynn Sparrow, Master Hypnotherapist and Dr. John Mein for teaching their unique style of hypnosis which helped me create my own style and vision in the production of this book.

SPECIAL ACKNOWLEDGEMENTS

I give a very special thank you to my dear friend, Patsy Sykes, Nationally Certified Hypnotherapist through the National Guild of Hypnotists. Patsy was instrumental in keeping the idea for Gaining Lightness alive. Her inspiration, motivation and insights were key in the finalization of this book. I commend Patsy for her many hours of reviewing the session material and for her skill in creating fresh ideas pertaining to the meditations/inductions, which are the crux of this being a successful program for all who use it. Patsy has been working with weight management clients for many years in her successful hypnotherapy practice at "Awakening Spirit" in Starkville, Mississippi.

I also want to thank Greg Sykes for playing his Native American-style flute music for the CDs used in this program. I'm sure you will find the music mesmerizing and inspiring as you go into and come out of the recorded meditations/inductions.

GAINING LIGHTNESS

INTRODUCTION

Not only is this the first day of the rest of your life, it's the first day of your new healthy life! You have embarked on a unique weight management program. It is designed to assist you in becoming lighter physically, mentally/emotionally and spiritually. I combine the mental and emotional components because as my favorite columnist, Marilyn vos Savant, so eloquently states "Feelings are what you get for thinking the way you do." It may be faulty thinking about your current dietary lifestyle that is creating the feelings you have about yourself. As a result of these feelings, you may not have been taking care of yourself in a manner that is best for your overall health. Hence, the unwanted weight is on and now the wait to do something about it is over.

There are many programs relating to weight management which will target the physical aspect of weight loss. But they are lacking in the other two important aspects of being, mind and spirit. Gaining Lightness is a multi-dimensional approach that will assist you in finding your "triggers" that up to now may have kept you from achieving your goals of attaining and maintaining the ideal weight for you. It is only through exploration of what those triggers are that will bring you into a position to make the changes you want to make now – permanently.

Triggers are those things, situations, or circumstances that instigate that need to eat. Some common triggers are stress over work, relationships, finances, etc.; boredom; guilt; loneliness; emptiness; and temptation. Triggers are then complicated with excuses like genetics (as in, do you fit in your genes?), being big-boned, culture, and time restraints that keep you from meal planning or exercise planning. You know now is the time to change all this. Just remember – if you always do what you always did, you'll always get what you always got! This concept can work against you, or now you can make it work for you.

THIS IS YOUR OPPORTUNITY TO BEGIN TO TIP THE SCALES IN YOUR FAVOR!

In order to make the comprehensive changes that will be optimal for you, Gaining Lightness is based on the idea of "chakras," or energy centers of the body. Chakra is an East Indian term that simply means "wheel," as in spinning wheel of energy – each being a vortex where energy flows into and out of the body. These chakras are interconnected by a vertical channel called sushumna, which allows movement of energy among the chakras. Each chakra has an associated color based on the energy vibration at each level.

You will be introduced to, or reminded of, the locations and the physical, mental/emotional and spiritual meanings of the seven major chakras associated with the body. And you will be guided in using these centers to bring balance and harmony to your entire life, i.e., homeostasis – the state of equilibrium between interrelated physiological, psychological and social factors. This is not meant to be esoteric in nature. It is simply a frame of reference to help you identify with and associate different aspects of your body in relation to health and imbalances. All of the chakras, when working together, keep us healthy and balanced in all aspects of our life.

Accordingly, these energy centers all relate to various aspects of your life. By focusing on each center and associating the areas of your life that are affected, you can begin to realize that your current weight may not be due to what you are eating, but rather what's eating you. As you work through each center, it will be easy for you to separate your current life experiences from the triggers that may have caused you to make less than desirable decisions on what and how much you eat. It is important that you work through the entire program in order to address all of your energy centers. You may have a preconceived notion as to which center is related to your issues, but there may be some that you are unaware of that are also contributing to your faulty eating, exercise and stress management patterns.

BASIC CHAKRA CONCEPTS

CONSIDER THE SYNOPSIS-STYLE INFORMATION REGARDING THE CHAKRAS ON THE FOLLOWING CHART:

Chakra	Location	Endocrine Gland	Psychological Function	Orientation to Self
1	Coccyx (tailbone)	Gonads	Survival	Preservation
2	Navel	Pancreas	Desire	Gratification
3	Solar Plexus	Adrenals	Control	Definition
4	Heart	Thymus	Love	Acceptance
5	Throat	Thyroid	Communication	Expression
6	Between eyebrows	Pituitary	Intuition	Reflection
7	Top of head	Pineal	Understanding	Knowledge

Note: Partially adapted from "Wheels of Life" by Anodea Judith

Imbalance within any of the chakras will have an impact on the physical health in the associated body area. For example, chakra 1 may be associated with sexual dysfunction, and problems with the hips, legs and feet; chakra 2 and 3 with digestive disorders; chakra 4 with heart and lung problems; chakra 5 may be associated with sore throats, coughs, etc.; chakra 6 with headaches, and sinus and eye problems; and chakra 7 may be related to endocrine or psychological imbalances. The following chapters will describe how any or all of these energy centers may be related to weight issues.

The Gaining Lightness program is designed to not only familiarize you with your energy centers, but also provide you with the tools to make them work most effectively for you in meeting your goals. Session one will introduce you to the overall concepts, while sessions two through eight will each focus on a specific chakra. Again, it is important that you work through the program in the order in which it is presented. You will be guided through each session with focused exercises, meditations and affirmations designed to help you meet your specific needs. The meditations and affirmations will be expressed through hypnosis.

Hypnosis is simply a trance or relaxation state in which you can access your subconscious mind to make the changes you want to make. While the term hypnosis is derived from the Greek God of Sleep, Hypnos, you will not be "asleep" during a hypnotherapy session. Rather, you will be in the state between wakefulness and sleep. The feeling is very similar to a deep meditation. Some people may actually believe they cannot be hypnotized. But virtually everyone has experienced the hypnotic states of daydreaming, being mesmerized by a dramatic movie or book, or having been driving down the highway and not remembering what exit they just passed, or where they were at that exact moment. Clearly, these are all varying states of hypnosis. We've all been there.

Hypnosis for some may be a scary thing. Due to the strange and sometimes embarrassing things that happen during stage hypnotism, which is what most people are accustomed to seeing, some individuals may fear being placed in a hypnotic trance. The ever entertaining "stage hypnotism" may put the fear into some people that they will be clucking like a chicken or barking like a dog, acting like they're fishing, or eating a thanksgiving dinner. The people doing these things on stage are the "hams" selected from the audience by the hypnotist and they would do these things whether they were hypnotized or not just to be the center of attention.

So, you can let go of the fear of loss of control. Actually, all hypnosis is self hypnosis and you are always in conscious control of your experience. You cannot and will not do anything under hypnosis that is against your moral principles, nor will you reveal secrets that you wouldn't share under normal circumstances.

Some people may have a fear of not coming out of the hypnotic state. Actually, there is no known record of anyone who has not been able to return to the "waking" state. Because all hypnosis is self hypnosis, you will be able to return fully to the conscious state at will. All you have to do is open your eyes and say mentally "I'm back!"

For each session, you will have a recorded meditation/induction to assist you in getting into that ideal state of relaxation to best help you facilitate the changes you want to make. The inductions are designed to inspire your imagination. Accordingly, they will address your subconscious mind which continues to have the childlike qualities of enjoying playfulness, fantasy and metaphor and will be delighted with the experience. The inductions are also printed in this text in case you feel that recording them in your own voice may be more effective. Either way, I'm sure you will be able to achieve your goals while figuring out exactly at what levels in your energy field your issues relate.

Goal setting is an important ingredient in attaining your ideal weight and fitness level. With some discipline, most people will drop 2 to 4 pounds per week on average. If you are carrying a lot of extra weight around, you may let go of up to 5 pounds or more in the first week, but find that most weeks you'll be in the 2 to 4 pound range. View yourself as successful even during weeks in which you let go of only one pound or hold steady. You didn't put the weight on overnight, so be patient in allowing yourself to gain lightness at your own pace. If you're looking for "another diet," you found it. Although this "diet" isn't precise on calorie or gram counting; it simply follows Webster's primary definition of diet which is "manner of living."

In reconstructing your "manner of living," consider making a contract style commitment to yourself. Such a commitment will certainly consume some of your time. But you are worth it! You know that if you had a friend in need, you wouldn't hesitate to give that person an hour or more of your time to be there for them. It's time to consider you as your own best friend and give yourself the time every day that will help you meet your goals. This will be a lifestyle in progress. You can make adjustments to your plan along the way. Be flexible! Give yourself the support you need to attain your goal and you will be successful! But before you commit to anything, I want to make sure your goals for Gaining Lightness are clear and your plan of action is do-able.

AS YOU DEVELOP YOUR PLAN OF ACTION, CONSIDER AS HONESTLY AND SPECIFICALLY AS POSSIBLE THE FOLLOWING QUESTIONS:

What do you want?

What will that do for you?

How will you know when you have it?

How will this affect other aspects (or people) in your life?

What stops you from having this already?

What resources do you already have that will help you obtain your outcome?

What additional resources do you need to obtain it?

How are you going to get there?

What's your first step?
Make it specific and achievable.

Is there more than one way to get there?

*Note: adapted from NFNLP Basic Practitioner Workbook

Perhaps you have quite a bit of weight to let go of and it would be in your best interest to establish interim goals to move you along until you reach your final goal destination. Coincidentally, in Neuro-Linguistic Programming, the term used for breaking down a huge goal into workable segments is called "chunking down." If your goal is to let go of all your undesired weight in a year, you can chunk it down to monthly goals or weekly goals. Just be realistic. You can revise your goal plan any time you want to make it work for you. The bottom line is that you are willing to change now.

Now that you're clear on your goals, please feel free to use the following contract of commitment, or compose your own which is tailor-made to your specific needs. Either way, you will be setting forth a plan of action to keep you on track. It may be in your best interest to read the commitment statement every day to firmly implant the ideas to apply to your daily activities.

CONTRACT/COMMITMENT

In the interest of self love and respect, I fully commit to bringing my body, mind and spirit into balance and harmony. I know this can be done easily by having a clear picture of the ideal me. It is time to honor me just because I am me. I currently and continuously forgive myself and others for whatever it is I need to release. As I let go of emotions and feelings which no longer serve me, I naturally let go of the weight that has accumulated as a result. Accordingly, I promise to take time for myself each day. I pattern my eating habits in such a way that I am Gaining Lightness by 2 to 4 pounds per week until I have reached my ideal weight. I use some form of exercising that is pleasing to me and engage in it at least 3 times per week. I continue to keep my mental and physical health a priority in my life to maintain the results I achieve. I follow the plan in this program by using the scripts or recordings on a daily basis. I determine at each level of the program what, if anything, I need to change that supports my goals. I continue to look forward to many more years of fun, fitness, health and happiness.

SIGNATURE

DATE

Having signed this contract of commitment, you have set the basic tenets for your new "manner of living"; your new way of life. It's a life of being physically active and being mindful of everything you consume; a life worth living as you begin Gaining Lightness!

HOW TO APPROACH THE
REMAINDER OF THIS BOOK

My recommendation is that you read the book one session at a time. That would be one session per week for eight weeks. After reading each session, chart your weight, and your current physical, mental, emotional and spiritual state. Then, listen to the CD related to the session. You can read the session content as often as you would like during the week, but I recommend that you take the time to listen to the CD everyday. Because you are serious about improving your body image, I'm sure you will find the time to take care of yourself.

> ALWAYS LISTEN TO THE CDS
> IN A SAFE, QUIET AND
> COMFORTABLE
> ENVIRONMENT. NEVER
> WHILE DRIVING A CAR OR
> OPERATING OTHER HEAVY
> EQUIPMENT.

GENERAL CONCEPTS

To focus on all aspects of health, it is necessary to incorporate body, mind and spirit. Accordingly, we can use the "triad of wellness" as a guide to ensure completeness in making all the changes necessary to create your ideal image.

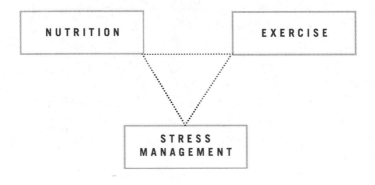

NUTRITION

Your digestive system is comprised of a structure called the alimentary canal. Alimentary means "to nourish." The alimentary canal is a tube that runs continuously from your mouth through the rectum to the anus and is about 20 to 30 feet long. Along the way are the pharynx (your throat), the esophagus, the stomach, the small intestines, and the large intestine otherwise known as the colon. This canal is where the process of ingestion, digestion, absorption and elimination occur.

Amazingly, the alimentary canal is hollow and if you straightened it out and blew it out, you'd be able to see right through it. Through the process of digestion and absorption, your digestive canal actually controls everything that is allowed to "enter" your body through the walls of the intestines and into the blood stream. Until your body accepts the nutrients from the canal, the food is not in you it is just traveling through you. Your body will selectively absorb all types of nutrients: vitamins and minerals, carbohydrates, proteins and fats. What your body absorbs and doesn't use is stored in your fat cells.

The hard fact is that you come into this life with a certain number (and you can bet it's a "shape-load") of fat cells – enough just for you and you never get anymore; so you go out of this life with the same number. The amount of fat you store in them is your choice (whether you believe it or not). You can choose to store enough fat to supply you with the right amount of energy and insulation you need; or you can choose to store enough for your neighborhood, your state, or a small third world country; but unfortunately, no one can use it but you.

In my certified personal training coursework, we used the book, "The Transition from Rehab to Fitness" by the International Sports and Fitness Trainers Association. The book listed the average daily recommended requirements for essential nutrients, i.e. protein = 30-40%; carbohydrates = 40-50%; and fats = 20-30%. Government labels regarding nutrition facts on many foods will aid you in following these guidelines. The bottom line is that you need fat, as well as protein and carbohydrates, in your diet to sustain balanced health. If possible, look for foods that are low in saturated fats. And when in doubt, go for high fiber, low fat foods. Also, beware of the "-ose's" like fructose, sucrose, dextrose, they're sugars. Look at the suffix "ose" as "Offsetting Success Efficiency." Read the nutrition labels on all the foods you buy.

While it may be helpful to check out nutrition labels on the foods you are buying, watch out for saboteurs like calorie counting or creating a "food diary." Calorie counting may seem like a good idea, but it may serve as permission to continue eating even after you are full; as in, "Gee, I have 50 calories left today, what can I eat?" Then you might eat one-fifth of a 250 calorie candy bar, but that other 4/5ths will haunt you for the rest of the evening. Using a food diary may be nice to use for a few days or so just for a reality check, but beyond that, by having to document everything you eat day in and day out will only serve to keep you focused on that which you want to control – food! If nutrition is a serious issue for you, it may be best for you to seek the services of a registered nutritionist to help you with meal planning and special dietary needs.

Up until now, you may have been tipping the scale in the wrong direction by overeating. Believe it or not, no food in and of itself can make you fat. The key is portion control. A serving size of potato chips is about 150 calories, which you could burn off easily just by driving your car for an hour. However, if you eat the entire 11 oz. bag, you'll ingest about 1,650 calories which sets up a whole other scenario for burning it off!

You may also fall into the pressure of "bad" foods and "good" foods. Again, no food in and of itself is either good or bad. Your perception of it makes it one or the other. Take for example, pizza. If you eat one personal pan style pizza with pepperoni, you will ingest about 675 calories. In the scheme of eating 3 meals a day, that's not really bad, especially if you drink plenty of water before and after your meal. In fact, the tomato sauce in that pizza contains lycopene, a powerful antioxidant which can reduce the risk of a variety of cancers.

Chocolate, which also gets a bad rap among "dieters," may be beneficial in moderate amounts. According to an article by the Institute for Natural Resources, chocolate contains phenylethyalanine which acts on the brain's mood centers giving us that "feel good" sensation. Chocolate also induces the release of endorphins, thereby elevating mood and reducing the perception of pain. The article goes on to say "as an additional enticement, chocolate (the dark variety in particular) contains antioxidants called catechins and polyphenols – the same antioxidants that are found in red wine and green tea." Antioxidants block the free radicals that interfere with normal cell reproduction and may also help reduce high blood pressure and LDL (low-density lipoprotein) cholesterol, often called "bad cholesterol."

Without too much creativity, you can apply these concepts to any foods that you care to eat. Just be aware of why you are eating them. Is it for some secondary gain for being overweight (e.g., protective shield, reduction of sexual threat, gain sympathy), emotional pacification; or is it perhaps just an oblivious stuffing? Being mindful of what you put into your body is an important aspect of weight management. Even high fat content delicacies such as Haagen-Dazs ice cream can be eaten without guilt because a 4 ounce serving only contains about 290 calories. Some treats are worth the calories because they taste so good.

Be aware that when you eat more than your body needs immediately and in the near future, the fat is stored in a variety of places in the body, and particularly in a structure called the greater omentum which covers your abdominal organs as part of the peritoneum. The greater omentum is attached to the bottom of the stomach and hangs down in front of the intestines. Its other edge is attached to the transverse colon. Also present in the abdomen is the lesser omentum which is attached to the top edge of the stomach and extends to the under surface of the liver. These drapings of fatty tissues are designed to give immediate energy to the surrounding organs like the liver and pancreas. They are not meant to be the primary source of energy for your entire body. Ironically, the "greater" the omentum, the more harmful it is for your body, particularly to those organs in the immediate abdominal region. The omenta are described as "thin" layers of fat; and for your best level of health they should remain that way.

Your stomach is about the size of a small fist and if you ate just enough to fill it comfortably you'd be eating an amount of food that would neatly fit into your cupped hands. Unfortunately (or not depending on your goals) the stomach will stretch to about three times its' resting size; but is it really worth the discomfort? Imagine how easy it might be to eat a comfortable amount of food if you use a smaller plate. This has a triple value – you get sufficient nutrition, you get the sense of completion, and it now becomes ok to eat everything on the plate.

You've probably heard a thousand times that breakfast is the most important meal of the day. Eat a healthful breakfast that includes protein and fiber and you may well be able to ward off hunger pangs later in the day. In their book "YOU on a DIET," Drs. Roizen and Oz relate that "Protein and fiber with high water content have a greater effect on satiety, and simple carbohydrates have the least effect on satiety.

(Fat, by the way, has an effect on satiety similar to that of protein and fiber, which is why lo-fat diets leave people hungry all the time.)" The authors also state: "If you can allow your body and brain to subconsciously do the work of controlling your eating, you'll naturally gravitate toward your ideal playing weight." This is where the power of hypnosis can be of great value to you. You will be relating your goals to your subconscious mind which through imagery will handle the details for you while monitoring your eating behaviors.

Just be careful of saboteurs such as buffets, or as I like to call them "puffets," because they'll puff you up – don't continue to eat just to "get your money's worth" (such places are usually quite cheap or reasonable anyway). Another example of a saboteur is "piggie sizing" your meals. Be aware that any type of super sizing your meals will only serve to super size you! "Super size" equals "super thighs" and later "super sighs" as you size up the damage. An ad for "all you can eat" should really send a red flag message your way. They'll tempt you with their incredible value; and again, most people will have a tendency to eat as much as possible to "get their money's worth." Instead, when eating out, consider splitting meals with a friend. Not only will you save money, you'll also save the unwanted calories. And rather than stuffing yourself with food at a meal, consider "doggie bags" or just leaving some food on your plate. Would you rather have the leftover food thrown in a garbage can, or would you like to be the garbage can? Oh, what a choice.

Lastly in the area of nutrition, drinking sufficient amounts of water should be a major consideration. Your body is made up of about 70% water. The digestive juices that break down your foods into usable molecules are 90%

water, and the lymph in your body which is critical to your immune system functioning protecting you against virus, bacteria and other pathogens contains a stunning 99% water. By drinking one or two glasses of water about a half hour prior to your meal, you set up the conditions in your stomach for efficient digestion and absorption of nutrients. Drinking another two glasses of water about 2 hours after the meal will help move the digested food to the small intestine for further processing.

A simple formula to determine the optimal amount of water for you is to divide your ideal body weight in half. That figure will give you a good idea in ounces how much water you should be drinking daily. Example: Ideal body weight of 130 pounds divided by 2 = 65. Ideally, you would consider drinking about eight 8-ounce glasses of water per day. Be realistic in this calculation and know that most sources recommend drinking 6 to 8 glasses of water each day. If you drink no water – and believe it or not some people drink no pure water in a day, drinking only coffee, tea, juices or soft drinks – build up your water intake gradually.

EXERCISE

From information I obtained in my ISFTA certified personal trainer program, I can assure you that exercise will be a major player in your ability to meet your weight management goals. Attempts at Gaining Lightness through dieting alone without adding any exercise depletes your muscle tissue stores. Muscle requires many calories each day just to maintain itself. The faster you lose weight through dieting alone, the more muscle tissue you lose. Exercise prevents muscle tissue loss and adds muscle to your body. The benefits of exercise include increased strength, increased flexibility, a more efficiently running metabolism, and efficiency in Gaining Lightness according to your goals.

Your body is designed for movement. That's why you have over 600 muscles. Ironically, the two strongest muscles in your body (ounce for ounce) are the masseter which is used for chewing, and the tongue which is used for tasting and swallowing. This doesn't mean that you should pay more attention to them. By exercising the other muscles of the body you can actually increase the effectiveness of your metabolism. Probably the most important muscles to exercise are your triceps on the back of your upper arms. These are the muscles you can use to push yourself away from the kitchen table.

Uh oh, I can almost hear you saying "I hate to exercise." This is a cop out. What are the real reasons you don't want to exercise? What are you afraid of? Could it be building muscle which weighs more than fat and the scale may not move like you want it to? Do you think you'll look silly because of the misconception that people your age don't exercise or do certain kinds of exercise? Or, you can't go to a gym until you look like a body builder for fear of embarrassment? Saying you belong to a gym isn't enough. It is of no value to exercise vicariously. "But I have a treadmill at home" you say, but it seems to be stuck in the corner and now has become a clothes rack. There's a popular ad on TV these days that says "Just do it." The truth is that you can't be in this physical body which is designed for movement and "hate" to move. There's something out there for everyone; yes, even you!

So, now it's decision time. Do you hate exercise less than you hate your current weight? Once you answer that question, you know what to do next – exercise! Exercise will help to increase the efficiency of your metabolism which is a key player as you begin Gaining Lightness! Metabolism is the amount of energy (calories) your body burns to maintain itself. It's a known fact that muscle uses more calories to maintain itself than fat.

HERE IS AN EXAMPLE OF THE APPROXIMATE NUMBER OF CALORIES YOU WILL BURN DURING AN HOUR OF THE FOLLOWING ACTIVITIES:

Aerobics	400
Backpacking	490
Bicycling	700
Calisthenics	320
Child care, sitting/kneeling	250
Child care, standing	560
Cleaning, general	250
Dancing	400
Gardening	350
Golf, carrying clubs	390
Golf, driving cart	250
Jogging	490
Mowing lawn	380
Sex	90
Stretching, e.g. hatha yoga	280
Swimming	500
Tai chi	280
Tennis	490
Volleyball	300
Walking	250
Weight lifting	250

Note: These previous figures are rounded and approximated from specific data found mostly on the website nutristrategy.com. Actual expenditure will depend on your specific weight and duration of the activity.

The amount of post-exercise elevation of metabolism (energy expenditure) depends on the intensity of exercise and to a lesser degree on the duration of exercise. Although, to get any real benefit from the exercise you perform, you'll want to do it for at least 20 minutes at a time. If you aren't currently exercising now, start off with 10 minutes and gradually build up to 30 minutes or more per day.

Only you can decide what is the best exercise for you – walking, running, aerobics, swimming, dancing, weight training, martial arts, Pilates, yoga – but whatever you do, commit to about 30 minutes per day 3 to 7 days per week. Find something that you really enjoy so that you will be motivated to stick with it. Doing exercises that you don't enjoy may actually be counterproductive to your goals because of the added stress it creates. Experiment if you don't currently have a favorite exercise; but you may want to consider including strength training, cardiovascular training, and stretching in your program. If you're considering going to a gym for your workouts, you may want to arrange some sessions with a certified personal trainer. A trainer will help you establish an exercise plan suited to your needs and ensure you are using the equipment correctly and safely. Or, there are thousands of exercise videos and community exercise programs to choose from. Doing anything is absolutely better than doing nothing.

Whatever you do, start off slowly and build up from there. If you already like to exercise, great!

**IF YOU CURRENTLY THINK YOU DON'T
LIKE TO EXERCIZE, AND THAT WAY OF
THINKING IS ALREADY BEGINNING TO
CHANGE, CONSIDER THE FOLLOWING
BENEFITS OF EXERCISE:**

- Increases calorie burning – both aerobic activity and strength training increase the number of calories you burn both during and after exercise.
- Increases the calories you burn at rest when you add more muscle to your body through strength training.
- Protects against muscle loss and adds muscle – some studies show that the weight you lose from dieting alone is 75% fat and 25% muscle. You want to lose as little muscle as possible to keep your metabolism elevated. Exercising regularly with strength training can prevent the muscle loss associated with dieting and can keep that metabolism running strong!
- Helps you eat less – exercise slows digestion and keeps you feeling full longer. It also helps maintain normalized blood glucose levels so you feel less hungry.
- Improves Self-Esteem – when you start feeling better about yourself and notice the positive psychological and physiological benefits exercise brings, it becomes easier and easier to stick with a (gaining lightness) program.
- Helps maintain (gained lightness) – research shows that the most critical factor in determining whether a person maintains (gained lightness) is whether he or she continues to exercise regularly.

Note: The previous information was adapted from information on the website thedietchannel.com. Whatever exercise plan you choose, remember to play in moderation. If you have a medical condition of any kind, consult your physician or other health care practitioner before starting your exercise program.

STRESS MANAGEMENT

George Burns was quoted as saying: "If you ask what is the single most important key to longevity, I would have to say it is avoiding worry, stress and tension. And if you didn't ask me, I'd still have to say it." Stress has been described as the experience during which the mind overrides the body's desire to beat the living daylights out of some idiot that desperately deserves it. Actually, it's the mind and body's reaction to something that is perceived as threatening or demanding. In regard to stress, perception is everything. Take for instance a roller coaster ride. The ride usually lasts one to two minutes. One person may get on the ride and experience high levels of exhilaration and can't wait to get back in line to do it again while another person will freak out just thinking about getting on the ride.

There are also two types of stress: eustress which is described as the "good stress"; and distress, usually associated with "bad stress." Both types of stress will produce similar physiological responses in the body. One might experience an increase in blood pressure, rapid heart rate, shallow rapid breathing, pupils dilating, heightened mental activity, an increase of blood flow to the skeletal muscles and the adrenal glands would start pumping out adrenaline and cortisol. During a eustress-type event, such as planning a wedding, the time leading up to the ceremony and the ceremony itself may be demanding (hopefully, not threatening e.g., shotgun wedding) and will produce a certain level of anxiety; and physiological responses may occur in varying degrees until the ceremony is completed. A distress event may be experienced if you're walking down a dark street and you see a group of rowdy thugs in your path. Personally, I'd cross the street or turn around and go the other way. But until I did, you might be able to imagine how my mind and body might react.

Such responses in the mind and body are defense mechanisms developed by our early ancestors. It's called the "fight or flight" response. Our nervous systems have two major branches – sympathetic and parasympathetic. The parasympathetic branch is our optimal state of rest, rejuvenation and repair. Being at this level is ideal for digestion, fighting off disease and illness, healing and dealing with life in general. The sympathetic branch is that with which we are motivated to action. It's not a bad thing. You need it to wake up in the morning, get out of bed and amble down for that first cup of coffee. It then carries you through your day dealing with whatever comes your way. It becomes a problem when you get to the "fight or flight" level and perhaps stay there for any extended period of time.

Fight or flight came into play for cave people to deal with frightening situations like being faced with a saber-toothed tiger. The choice was to fight or run away. So, the sympathetic nervous system kicked in, blood rushed to the skeletal muscles so they could club the beast or take off running; the pupils dilated so they would become hyper-vigilant and be able to take in the surroundings to look for safety; and the mind would race to find the appropriate response – all for the sake of survival. Once the cave person went through the process of any course of physical action, the adrenaline and cortisol would dissipate, and the body would go back into parasympathetic mode. (Stress reduction is so easy a cave man can do it.)

In today's times, we still have the same type of physical and mental stress responses. The trouble is that fighting or fleeing may not be viable options. Say for instance, your boss comes in to your office and begins to yell at you because you are late in turning in a very important report. Your options aren't to club the boss or run away. So, you have to come up with reasonable alternatives to get the body back into the parasympathetic state. The problem with most of us is that we get into these situations, feel the stress and then just blow it off as "Oh, I can deal with that" without taking any steps to get back to a normal state. And then, something else happens producing the same stress response and you just pile it on. And again, and again, and again until one day you reach your absolute limit and you pop!

It is natural for your body to produce adrenaline and cortisol to handle short and long term stressful situations. Cortisol is produced by the adrenal glands and is necessary for proper glucose metabolism, regulation of blood pressure, proper immune functioning, and the body's inflammatory response. When it appears in the body in over abundance it may cause impaired mental functioning, suppressed thyroid function, blood sugar imbalances, lower immune system functioning, higher blood pressure, and decreased bone density and muscle tissue.

It is ideal to have a consistent pattern of activity and rest, allowing you to stay at an optimal level of functioning. When you pile on stress without doing anything to relieve it, all kinds of things may begin to happen. You may find yourself eating when you're not hungry, eating without even tasting the food, and experiencing physiological problems e.g., headaches, nausea, fatigue, irritability, insomnia, tight muscles, high blood pressure, depression and an inability to focus – and that's just the short list. While you're in that fight or flight mode, two very important systems of the body are suppressed – digestive and immune. Relating this back to cave person days, the body doesn't care if you digested that last meal if you may die in the next two minutes. Similarly, your body doesn't care if it fights off those bacteria, virus or other pathogens now if you're going to die in the next few minutes. You need to get back into the parasympathetic mode of functioning for those systems to kick back in.

One of the quickest ways to get from the sympathetic nervous system state of fight or flight to the parasympathetic state is through deep breathing. This is also called abdominal or diaphragmatic breathing. That's because as you take the deep breaths, your diaphragm muscle will contract causing your abdomen to protrude, increasing the volume capacity in your thorax for lung expansion. I'm sure you've been told that when you are really stressed out or angry you should count to ten. What tends to happen is that we will go 1-2-3-4-5-6-7-8-9-10 rapidly and say something like, "I'm still mad!"

The real concept behind this is to count to ten using deep breathing. Try it. Place your hand on your abdomen so you can feel it move. Then, inhale slowly and deeply through your nose and exhale slowly through your mouth or nose as you tighten your abdominal muscles and count "one." Inhale…exhale, following the same pattern and count "two." Inhale…exhale, "three." You are probably already beginning to feel a state of calmness, so you can imagine what you would feel like and how relaxed you'd be after reaching a count of ten.

Now that you've learned how to breathe effectively, you're probably beginning to wonder why up until now you've been having problems focusing; you can't control your appetite; you're tired all the time; you have irritable bowel syndrome; you're experiencing muscle pain or headaches; and you get sick all the time. If so, and you can add any negative thing that's happening to you that may not appear on this list, you may continue to wonder what it is that you are doing to yourself. Part of it may be your response to stress.

According to Murphy's Law of Thermodynamics, things get worse under pressure. But Murphy, in my opinion, is a pessimist. We, on the other hand, are optimists! We see life's crises the way the Chinese characters for crisis have been said to describe it – danger/challenge and opportunity. I have a friend who when others would ask how he's doing would respond: "Fantastic! Every day's a new day of challenge and opportunity." What a great way to look at life. Anyone can change their outlook on life and commit to handle it in a new way. Consider Reinhold Niebuhr's words: "God grant me the serenity to accept the things I cannot change, the courage to change the things I can, and the wisdom to know the difference." By cultivating serenity, courage and wisdom you will be able to deal with any situation effectively and with a minimal amount of stress.

Stress management may be partly accomplished through nutrition and exercise. Nutrition and exercise are primarily associated with the physical level. Although, one could argue that good nutrition will nourish the body, mind and spirit. While exercise is an excellent way to release those "feel-good" chemicals – endorphins which contribute to a calm, relaxed mind and spirit, there are many other ways to reduce your stress levels. Other methods for reducing stress are reading, shopping (until the bills arrive), working on a hobby such as gardening, quilting, woodworking, and through meditation. In the meditations (in hypnosis, they're called inductions) used in this book, you will not be asked to totally clear your mind. Rather, the inductions will guide you to focus on relaxation and contemplation, and on manifesting the goals to which you are committed. Your chakras will also be used as a focal point to facilitate your change.

CONTINUING ON

As each of the following sessions will deal with a specific chakra, just be aware for now that these energy centers simply relate to the following:

CHAKRA 1 Located at the base of the spine relates to safety/security issues.
COLOR IS RED

CHAKRA 2 Located at the navel relates to relationships.
COLOR IS ORANGE

CHAKRA 3 Located at the solar plexus relates to personal power/control.
COLOR IS YELLOW

CHAKRA 4 Located behind the breastbone relates to unconditional love.
COLOR IS GREEN

CHAKRA 5 Located at the throat relates to self expression, will and communication.
COLOR IS BLUE

CHAKRA 6 Located between the eyebrows relates to intuition and purpose.
COLOR IS INDIGO.

CHAKRA 7 Located at the crown of the head relates to your conceptualization of divine spirit.
COLOR IS VIOLET

Coincidentally enough, these levels of being basically follow the psychologist Abrahm Maslow's hierarchy of needs, i.e. safety, belongingness, need for affection and self actualization. So if these concepts seem esoteric, you are asked to let go of your pre-conceived notions about them and begin to know that they are important to achieving your goals.

In her book, "Anatomy of the Spirit," Caroline Myss describes the chakras as sources of energy that are designed to serve the body, mind and spirit. By focusing your attention (energy) on those situations that are happening to you or disturbing you, energy goes out to those things and is not available for you, or the organs in the associated body area! She discusses the concept of "calling your spirit back" in order to bring your whole being back into balance. The tools that follow will assist you in recognizing those areas where you are expending excess energy and help you in restoring your energy reserves.

As you go through the program, you are asked to consider for each chakra those areas of your life that may have contributed to your being the weigh you are now and how you might make the changes necessary to be the weigh you want to be. It is important that you explore each area thoroughly. Only then will you be able to assess at what level you began to protect yourself by building walls, stuffing yourself with faulty ideas, filling yourself with food to replace the love you may not be experiencing, or swallowing that which may be easier to ingest than the words you might have said or that which is happening in your life.

These concepts are not meant to be overly simplistic. Only you know why it is that you have attained the weight you are now. You may know it at the conscious level. But if you don't, you will know it at the subconscious level. That's where hypnosis comes into play most effectively. You will be assisted in identifying those aspects of your life that contributed to your current size, and in letting go of the energy of those things so that you may easily and effectively get to where you want to be. In effect, you will be "tipping the scales in your favor."

All throughout this program, you will be assisted in creating affirmations that will be life changing. There are three primary components to phrasing affirmations: they should be personal, present, and positive. Accordingly, your affirmations will almost always begin with "I." To keep them in the present, use the words such as "am," "have," or "always." Keeping your affirmations phrased positively will help you focus on what you want, not on what you don't want; hence the phrase, "You can't not think about what it is you don't want to think about without thinking about it first." For example, don't think about how good you'll look and feel after attaining your ideal weight. I'll bet you just did mentally what I told you not to do. That's because your mind has to process the negative before it can take any action on what it is you do want. (In this case, the action you were asked not to think about is what you want, but you get the point, right?) In contrast, the affirmation "I want to be my ideal weight" will keep you "wanting" to be your ideal weight. The affirmation "I don't want to be fat" will always keep you "wanting" not to be fat! Rather, try the affirmation, "I am at my ideal weight." Or, "I enjoy the perfect kinds and quantities of food that allow me to attain and maintain my ideal weight."

Louise Hay's books are a wonderful resource for affirmations. While you can use those affirmations and the affirmations presented in this book effectively as they are written, you may find it more beneficial to tailor them to meet your specific needs. Doing this will make them more true to your own conscious and subconscious minds, and make them even more effective in meeting your goals.

BEFORE LISTENING TO THE SESSION 1 CD, CHECK IN AND RECORD YOUR CURRENT STATE OF HEALTH:

My current weight is _____ pounds.

As of this writing, this is how I feel:

Physically:

Mentally:

Emotionally:

Spiritually:

SESSION TWO:

CHAKRA 1- ROOT CHAKRA

RED

The Root Chakra, located at the base of the spine relates to safety, security and basic survival needs. Questions to ask yourself to help determine if you have issues related to the Root Chakra include: Do you have enough money to meet your needs? Do you feel secure in your current job, or your ability to get one? Do you know where your next meal is coming from? Do you feel secure in your relationship(s)? When finding that basic needs are not met through life experiences, some people have the tendency to irrationally try to meet those needs in other, not necessarily functional, ways.

Through your up-bringing, you may have been subjected to the concept that you needed to "clean your plate" and if you didn't, less fortunate children in other countries may suffer due to your irresponsibility. Like your not eating all the food on your plate may make these children suffer even more, or this act may affect the availability of food for others in the world. While food is important to survival, as in some areas of life, more is not necessarily better.

Believe it or not, our bodies can survive on a minimal amount of food. The key here, as in everything we experience, moderation is an absolute necessity. There are hundreds, if not thousands, of "diets" you can follow to maintain your ideal weight. You may be inspired to follow the food pyramid which is touted by the FDA and other organizations which propose a life of balance in eating choices. Some books will tell you, diets don't work! My belief in this regard is that by following the concept of "everything in moderation, including moderation," any program will work if you really want it to.

So, what is it at this energy level that makes us gain weight? Fear? When you look at our society realistically, you can not starve. Even if you don't have money to buy food, there are social programs, church programs and community programs in place that will ensure that you will have all the food you need to survive. Food is absolutely necessary for survival. Ironically, rats in scientific studies that were given only sufficient food to sustain life, or were considered "underfed," were less prone to disease and lived longer than those that were overfed.

Another fear may be related to ridicule or guilt from family members. The family or other social groups in relation to the root chakra has been described by many as the "tribe." How does your tribe usually eat at holidays or other family gatherings? The tribal festivities I've attended almost always include feasts of all kinds of main dishes and desserts. How many times have you eaten way more than you really wanted so you wouldn't hurt the feelings of those who brought food to the gathering? What's happened to me, and perhaps you can relate, is that I've just finished eating what I felt was a reasonable amount of food and someone says, "Oh, you have to try my dessert. It's Great Grandma Bertha's special recipe and everybody just loves it!" Then you're stuck with the dilemma of eat it or be eaten alive with ridicule, guilt or shame from all those at the event who love and miss Great Grandma Bertha.

Even when someone dies, you can't avoid it. Now you host, or want to (or have to) attend a "wake" after the ceremonies, which from my experience always includes a ton of food. At this event, it is presumed that one needs to fill the void resulting from the loss of a loved one with food. If you go just to fill your emotional needs through conversation and bonding, others will look at you as if you had the plague if you don't eat, or as is expected by the tribe, eat a lot. The implied message is that Uncle Joe's passing must not be that important to you, or you are lacking in emotional expression.

Have you ever experienced a guilt trip? It's that experience of fearing you did something you "shouldn't" have, or didn't do everything you "should" have done. There will probably never be a lack of people who will try to make you feel like you're wrong, responsible for something that went wrong or didn't live up to those things they thought you should have or could have done in a certain situation. And if there aren't enough of these people around some of us will have the tendency to do it to ourselves. Know anyone like that? You may even feel guilty about what you eat, especially in front of others. This can set up the condition of sneaking food or hiding food so no one else will get it; and it's there just for you – the infamous closet eating syndrome.

To me, guilt means: Giving Up Independence through Limiting Thoughts. You can always change your thoughts that may cause negative feelings when someone says something hurtful or imposing to you. A response to the Great Grandma Bertha scenario might go like: "You know, I love Great Grandma Bertha and she does have some wonderful recipes; how about if you wrap a piece up for me so I can enjoy it later." This way, you assert that you are still part of the tribe and you can decide later whether to eat or discard the dessert. If you truly like it, eat it; or at least part of it if you were given a giant serving. You'll find it easier and easier to keep your goals for Gaining Lightness foremost in your mind.

The root chakra is also associated with sexual satisfaction. Bluntly, are you getting enough? We all have a varying degree of sexual needs. No one can say how much is enough for you, but you. However, in your heart, you know whether or not you are satisfied now. And everyone knows that quality, not quantity will be the best measure of meeting needs. Needs that are not met in the way intended will be met through other means. In fact, any emptiness can seemingly (yet, dysfunctionally) be filled with food. Although, satisfaction is not guaranteed! Even though you may have that full feeling, your need is not adequately fulfilled; therefore, you fall into that vicious cycle that unfortunately has no completion and you continue to consume that which cannot realistically meet the need. If it is a sexual hunger that needs to be filled, explore with your mate ways to make intimacy more fulfilling. If you're not currently in relationship, remember the phrase "it takes two to tango" pertains only to dancing.

The key here is to be ok with yourself here and now the way you are sexually, financially, relationship-wise, job-wise, etc. and realize that none of these aspects of your life can actually control you. Just know that everything in your life has the propensity to be different than it is now. Creating affirmations that project the way you want to be in the tense that you already have it, will assist you in achieving everything you want to be different in your life.

SOME EXAMPLES OF ROOT CHAKRA AFFIRMATIONS ARE:

I am secure in my life as it is.

My work life is filled with abundance and prosperity.

I know that I always have enough to eat to sustain life and healthful living.

I develop and maintain relationships that support my physical, mental/emotional and spiritual well-being.

I am secure and grounded in this physical form.

BEFORE LISTENING TO THE SESSION 2 CD, CHECK IN AND RECORD YOUR CURRENT STATE OF HEALTH:

My current weight is _____ pounds.

I have been successful at Gaining Lightness by letting go of _____ total pounds!

As of this writing, this is how I feel:

Physically:

Mentally:

Emotionally:

Spiritually:

CHAKRA 2 - NAVEL CHAKRA

ORANGE

Chakra 2 located at the area of the navel is associated with relationships. This can be any kind of relationship: parents, spouse, siblings, friends, co-workers, pets, food and most importantly, yourself. And, you might begin to wonder how each of these relationships is working out for you. Do you get along with one or some better than others? How have your relationships with others affected the way you look at food and eating?

One of the aspects of relationships is that sometimes they end; like having a parent pass on or a friend die. (Of course this can happen with pets too.) Others may experience separation or divorce. You may have lost your job and are no longer part of the group of workers that you perceived as your friends. You may have moved to another location or another state. Some people may tend to see this loss as leaving an emptiness inside. Then typically, the next step to deal with an emptiness is to fill it. Up until now, it may have felt quite natural to fill that void with food. But, does food really do the job you intended it to do? Perhaps it did fill you physically; however, that is not the real need asking for attention.

Probably instead, it was an emotional or psychological need that had to be met. Strangely enough there seems to be some connection, but really, there isn't. You may have, up until now, had a faulty thinking pattern which followed the thought that if X is empty, Y can fill it. That thinking is great if X is your stomach and Y is food; but if X is a loss of some aspect of relationship in your life (creating an emotional emptiness), then physiologically, Y (food) can't fill the void.

Unfortunately, you can't fill an emotional need with a physical substance. You may have tried this in the past, but look what it has done for you. Big results, right? But I'm sure they're not the results you originally anticipated or wanted. You can fill the emotional needs with things like positive self-talk through affirmations or by talking through your issues with someone you trust. You may even fill that void by establishing new rewarding relationships.

All of these coping devices play a role in creating your eating patterns. Typically, you don't eat the same foods or in the same manner that your pets do unless you've been following some strange diet program that I haven't read about yet. But chances are you experience some of the same eating patterns that your friends or family members have. These patterns may be as simple as overeating at picnics or holiday events. Or, you may have experienced faulty eating patterns on a daily (or 3 times daily) basis with your spouse or other family members. It's the simple "monkey see, monkey do" syndrome. And you may begin to imagine why it is that these folks are fat too.

As you approach, or are in, your adult years, your conversations regarding food may have moved from the "clean your plate" phenomenon to phrases like "a moment on the lips, a lifetime on the hips"; or when you see a giant dessert, you may say something like "I may as well just slap this on my thighs; it's going to end up there anyway." And, knowing these concepts intimately, you eat the stuff anyway because getting fat is inevitable, right? No freakin' way!

Fortunately for you, you are beginning to do something about these faulty patterns. You're beginning to look at your eating patterns in a new light. Your mind may have been full of old triggers that are like roots. Unfortunately, those roots are attached to the weeds that tend to grow and push out, or kill off, the functional vegetation that belongs in your garden of emotions. By mentally weeding, you can create a space of fresh start for the new growing season. And you can see yourself growing into a healthy, happy person who tills the garden in such a way that only the healthiest, freshest growth occurs. That is, growing strong bones, strong muscles, a strong attitude toward health and fitness, and a strong new relationship with yourself.

You may have been told that people can't change because a leopard can't change its spots or some other faulty logic. Well, excuse my French but "cela est la foutaise" which means "that's not true," kind of. You can change your relationship with yourself. Begin seeing yourself in a new light, kind of like Gaining Lightness in your mind. Let go of those negative thought patterns that have been weighing you down, such as self-criticism (remember Rodney Dangerfield who said "I would never join a club that would have me as a member."), or criticism by others, unrealistic expectations imposed on you by yourself or others; and begin to recognize those good qualities you have.

Honor your strengths. Regardless of what you may have been told up to this point, everyone has them, including you. I'm sure you can think of at least one time in your life where you were successful, achieving your goals. What are you really good at? (No copping out here, everybody is good at something). Look at up to this point how good you were at putting yourself down or cleaning your plate. Just think how powerful it will be to turn that energy around and use it in functional ways. What have you done for others and what good qualities do they see in you that you can incorporate into your own self concept?

A great line from the movie "Coach Carter" goes: "Our greatest fear is not that we are inadequate (or insignificant). Our deepest fear is that we are powerful beyond measure. It is our light, not our darkness that most frightens us. Your playing small does not serve the world. There is nothing enlightened about shrinking so that other people won't feel insecure around you. We were all meant to shine as children do. It's not just in some of us, it's in everyone. And, as we let our own light shine, we unconsciously give other people permission to do the same. As we are liberated from our own fear, our presence automatically liberates others."

AFFIRMATIONS RELATED TO THE NAVEL CHAKRA MAY BE PHRASED LIKE THIS:

I nourish only those relationships that support my goals.

I grow emotionally stronger everyday.

I fill my emotional voids with love.

I am continually developing healthy relationships.

I express my sexuality and creativity with joy.

BEFORE LISTENING TO THE SESSION 3 CD, CHECK IN AND RECORD YOUR CURRENT STATE OF HEALTH:

My current weight is _____ pounds.

I have been successful at Gaining Lightness by letting go of _____ total pounds!

As of this writing, this is how I feel:

Physically:

Mentally:

Emotionally:

Spiritually:

SESSION FOUR:
CHAKRA 3 - SOLAR PLEXUS

YELLOW

This is the chakra of transformation.

The area around the base of the sternum is called the solar plexus. It relates to a bundle of nerves that innervates the abdominal region and branches out in all directions much like the rays of the sun and hence gets its name. The third chakra relates to personal power. It's like the "control" center. The energy of this chakra may be depleted by you giving up control to other people or things – like food.

Did you ever have the feeling that you were out of control with food? It's just sitting there minding its own business and somehow beckons you over to check it out and then, of course, eat it. (Consider the old familiar saying – "out of sight, out of mind"; take control!) You may have found yourself mindlessly chomping down on this food that you really didn't want in the first place, may not have even tasted it, and somehow now it's gone – consumed. What do you think may have caused this scenario?

You have given your power, or control away. This behavior probably isn't limited to just food. You are probably feeling powerless or out of control in other areas of your life too. Maybe in your job you are stripped of your personal power because you have a boss who wants you to just do whatever she or he says without any input from you, regardless of how viable your ideas may be for program or production efficiency. Or, did anyone ever "put" you on a guilt trip and you either didn't do something you wanted to or acquiesced to their demands? Can anyone really put you on a guilt trip? Really, think about that!

So, how much control do you have in your job, in your relationships with people, and especially in your relationship with food? As far as your job goes, if you're not loving it, just the stress of going to work every day and dealing with the people and problems may be pushing you over the edge with excessive eating – which is a dysfunctional coping strategy by the way. Did you ever consider that it might be to your benefit to think about finding another job that you would truly enjoy; which would fill the "belongingness" or "achievement" needs that you desire. I have talked with some people who stay in jobs or relationships they hate because they feel like they don't have a choice. If this sounds like you, it's time to get in touch with your third chakra, the chakra of personal power and find a way to make the changes you need to create a more satisfying life. In other words, choose a more ideal life or lifestyle. You always have a choice!

Similarly, most people can choose with whom they establish relationships. Depending on proximity of family members or the type of job you have, these relationships may continually be in your face. But you can choose how you let these people affect you. When considering maintaining relationships with people who support your goals, think about their eating habits and how they might affect you. If you were a recovered alcoholic, you wouldn't hang out with heavy drinkers. Or, if you recently became a non-smoker, you probably wouldn't associate with heavy smokers on a regular basis. You can see where this is going, right? Once you've attained your goals for Gaining Lightness, you may effectively reestablish some of these relationships with little impact on your behavior because your new path is clear.

Some people will actually blame their eating on other

people, or situations outside themselves. Your Aunt Bessie says "Is that all you're having? You eat like a bird!" Or the waitress says (while holding a tray of mouth watering delights) "Did you save room for dessert?" You've just eaten enough to feed a family of four, but she waves that dessert tray under your nose and your eyes, and all of a sudden you feel like you can defy physics and you order it. Once you place the blame elsewhere, you've placed the control outside of you. "It's not my fault" you whine. At the risk of you throwing this program in the trash, (another out-of-control act) I'll argue that the fault is yours. Unless someone ties you down and continually stuffs food in your mouth and makes you swallow it, somewhere within you is the personal power to monitor everything you eat and control the quality and quantity of food that you consume. Consider the following short story:

AUTOBIOGRAPHY IN FIVE SHORT CHAPTERS
By Portia Nelson

1. I walk down the street.
> There is a deep hole in the sidewalk.
> I fall in.
> I am lost......I am hopeless.
> It isn't my fault.
> It takes forever to find a way out.
2. I walk down the same street.
> There is a deep hole in the sidewalk.
> I pretend I don't see it.
> I fall in again.
> I can't believe I am in the same place.
> But it isn't my fault.
> It still takes a long time to get out.
3. I walk down the same street.
> There is a deep hole in the sidewalk.
> I see it is there.
> I still fall in......it's a habit.
> My eyes are open
> I know where I am.
> It is my fault,
> I get out immediately.
4. I walk down the same street.
> There is a deep hole in the sidewalk.
> I walk around it.
5. I walk down another street.

You have the ability to choose your new path now;
the path to Gaining Lightness!

And then, there's the ego. The third chakra is where your ego lies. The ego is that part of you that wants you to continue to live. It will do anything it can to sustain life. Part of sustaining life is eating. You and your ego know that you need to eat in order to feed each and every one of your cells. But how much does each cell need to continue to live? The ego actually doesn't care. So, it may tell you at some level that you need to develop a store house of food (energy) to ensure that life continues. Are you aware that you control the ego, and not vice versa? The third chakra also gives you the power to control all aspects of your life.

What the third chakra boils down to is self esteem, or how you regard yourself. No one wants to be a loser and that's one reason this program is titled "Gaining Lightness." It's about letting go of those things (the heaviness) that no longer serve you and about gaining new behaviors and ideas that will keep you feeling good about yourself. When you gain control of the situations and behaviors that somehow got you to where you are now, i.e. the weigh you are, you empower yourself to gain control of all aspects of your life.

Self esteem is affected by past programming whether it was positive or negative. If your past has been blessed with all positives about you – your successes, achievements, good looks, great body, etc. – that's great. But if you have been subjected to negative programming or judgments by your parents, siblings, classmates, teachers, co-workers, or even your "friends" those statements may be negatively affecting your current self perception.

Being called such things as lazy, clumsy, fat, ugly, stupid, or bad may be having a negative impact on you now at the conscious or subconscious level. Self defeating thoughts like "nobody cares about or loves me" or "diets don't work for me" will continue to keep you from your goals until you begin now to let go of those thought patterns and set yourself free. And then, you might ask yourself "Are these things really true or are they just excuses?" You know that there's at least one person out of the 6 billion people on this planet that cares about or loves you; and what is it about you that doesn't allow diets to work for you?

Well-meaning people, (well kind of well-meaning) may unknowingly sabotage your progress. I remember going to a family reunion a while back after letting go of about 10 pounds of the 40 pounds I was intending to drop and I was feeling pretty good about myself until an uncle came up to me, poked me in the stomach and asked "When are you due?" (I'm a guy, remember?) You can imagine what thoughts may have been going through my head after that "well-meaning" remark – thoughts of failure; even though I had already successfully reached one-fourth of my goal.

Based on scenarios from your past, or even from others' past performance, you may be feeling a fear of failure. After a time when you didn't quite meet your goal, or accomplish something you were expected to do, did you ever hear "I told you so," or "I knew you couldn't do it?" Fear of success is just as common. Anticipation of continued success may cause stress or anxiety due to having to keep up a certain pace, certain expectation, or it may be counterproductive in relation to the secondary gains you get from non-change.

Such conditions may also set up a fear of change which can cause you to choose to procrastinate. You know the concept, "Why do today what you can put off until tomorrow?" Procrastination, in effect is a loss of control. It may simply be a matter of misdirected priorities. And yes, it is a choice. I'm sure there are many times in your life when you were motivated to do something on a moments notice and chose to work on it immediately. They were undoubtedly things you really wanted to do – like preparing for and being on time for a job interview for a position you really wanted, or completing a project such as remodeling a room in your house because having that new look is very pleasing for you. You're probably wondering right now how pleasing your new look will be to you as you continue Gaining Lightness. How well are you meeting your goals?

You know where you are and where you want to be. You hold the power and self-control in your solar plexus chakra; you hold the power to make all the changes you want to make. It's time for that change now!

Self acceptance is where it's at and there's no better place to start than where you are now. You can begin to set yourself free by thinking about the successes you have experienced in your life; about all the people in your life who do care about you, appreciate you and support you; or about times when you were capable of using your strengths for endured accomplishment. What you focus your attention on will expand or manifest in your life. An appropriate quote from Napoleon Hill states, "There is one quality that one must possess to win, and that is definiteness of purpose, the knowledge of what one wants and a burning desire to achieve it." Feel that desire now!

IT MAY BE HELPFUL TO USE SOLAR PLEXUS AFFIRMATIONS LIKE:

I eagerly gain control of all aspects of my life.

I lovingly accept myself and all the good I am capable of.

I am free of all negative thought patterns.

I recognize my personal power and use it to attain my goals.

BEFORE LISTENING TO THE SESSION 4 CD, CHECK IN AND RECORD YOUR CURRENT STATE OF HEALTH:

My current weight is _____ pounds.

I have been successful at Gaining Lightness by letting go of _____ total pounds!

As of this writing, this is how I feel:

Physically:

Mentally:

Emotionally:

Spiritually:

SESSION FIVE:
CHAKRA 4 - HEART

GREEN

Unconditional love is the concept associated with the heart chakra. This is love beyond "If you'll do this or that for me, I'll love you." I wonder if you can even imagine what unconditional love might be or feel like. If you ever had a dog (or knew someone who has) you might have experienced unconditional love. It seems that no matter what you do to the dog, it adores you like nothing has ever happened. You can leave it alone, ignore it and God forbid, even kick it (we'll discuss transference later) and the dog will come at you with even more love and devotion than before. I'm not suggesting that you get a dog, although it might be nice to have one around to eat all the leftover scraps that up until now you have been so inclined to eat.

In the classes I teach, I often ask students if they love themselves. And, they'll undoubtedly respond "Of course I do." Then I take it one step further and ask if they love themselves unconditionally. Then I usually just get "that look"; you know the one I mean. To test whether or not you have unconditional love for yourself, try this. Strip down naked and stand in front of a full length mirror, look yourself in the eyes and say "I love you." Do this without judgment on all levels. Ignore the fact that you are bulging in a variety of places, you have committed some past indiscretions and you have not cared for yourself in a way in which you deserve; then, notice how that feels.

Now, do you think that if you truly loved yourself unconditionally that you would be the weigh you are now? This body you were given needs lots of love, care and maintenance to last you a lifetime – however long that might be for you. You know that the better you take care of your body, the better you'll feel and probably the longer it will last. (Mickey Mantle was quoted as saying: "If I knew I was going to live this long, I would have taken better care of myself.") And you're probably well aware of how being overweight or obese might affect your quality or length of life. If you're drawing a blank, let me remind you.

According to the American Obesity Association, about 65% of Americans are categorized as overweight or obese. Obesity causes about 300,000 deaths in the U. S. each year; and annual health care costs of American adults with obesity amount to about $100 billion. Additionally, obesity has been shown to increase the risks of arthritis, certain types of cancers, cardiovascular disease, type 2 diabetes, high blood pressure, infertility, liver disease, and strokes, to name a few. Can you feel the love? And you thought you had nothing to look forward to.

I didn't put this information in here to scare you (well, ok, just a little), but rather to motivate you to take charge of your life now. You can start by telling yourself everyday that you love you unconditionally – and mean it! Then, it will become easier and easier for you to do those things you need to in order to continue Gaining Lightness. You know, exercise, eat right and change your attitude about stress.

One very nice way to let go of stress in the heart chakra is to begin to practice forgiveness. The first step will be to forgive yourself for anything you may have done up until now that contributed to your weight gain. Remember, you can only do what you know how to do. In the past, you were only doing what you knew how to do. But now, you have new resources to change your behaviors and continue on your path to Gaining Lightness.

There may also be people in your distant or recent past who you "blame" for your current condition and eating habits. Whatever these people "did" to you is not the cause of your being overweight. It's how you let what they said or did affect you that's the real problem. You may have been in a family that was into big meals. I've eaten with families like that and if you try to leave the table after having only one serving, you get ridiculed for "eating like a bird" and pressured into eating more than you really want. And then, of course, there's always dessert which is homemade from scratch and you just have to try it – or else! (Guilt trip) These people are not the problem, so allow yourself to go inside your head and inside your heart and forgive them. Or, as discussed previously, you may have been hurt emotionally by someone and tried to stuff down the pain, or fill the void that was left with food. Again, these people are not the problem, so allow yourself to go inside your head and inside your heart and forgive them.

To forgive is not always to forget. Thomas Szasz once said "The stupid neither forgive nor forget; the naïve forgive and forget; the wise forgive but do not forget." That's because like George Santayana said, "Those who cannot remember the past are doomed to repeat it." On your path to Gaining Lightness, you don't want to forget those things, people or situations that contributed to causing you to eat mindlessly or excessively because you don't want to repeat those old patterns. But, it may be in your best interest to forgive them so you can release the power they once had over you.

In reality, they have no power over you. You, through the concept of transference, may have taken emotions that should have been directed at some person or situation; but because it didn't feel safe to express them in that direction, you transferred the emotion inward because that seemingly may have caused you less trouble. You can see how that behavior might cause you more trouble personally in the long run. If you can stand one more quote here, Alexander Pope once said, "To err is human; to forgive, Divine." Accept your divinity at the heart chakra and begin forgiving. My recommendation is to start by forgiving yourself and go from there.

IN ONE OF MY HYPNOTHERAPY CLASSES, DR. ALLEN CHIPS PRESENTED HIS CORE VALUES GRID:

Victim of   Path of
Circumstances   Perfection

Where do you see yourself on this grid? At the Victim end of the grid, a person might hold negative beliefs about themselves and others which are driven by victim roles. For these people, life just happens and they "play the hand they're dealt." The person on the Path of Perfection end will feel more self empowerment and see the purpose behind every experience. George Elliott said "It's never too late to be what you might have been."

Remember when I asked you to strip naked and look into a full length mirror and try to view yourself without judgment? The Victim of Circumstances will stand there like the character Eeyore (it's funny, "spell check" didn't recognize this name and humorously recommended that this word be changed to "eye sore"), saying something like "Oh me, oh my." In the Winnie the Pooh book Eeyore was standing by the side of a stream and looked at himself in the water. "Pathetic," he said. "That's what it is, pathetic." He turned and walked to the other side of the stream, looked at himself in the water again and said, "As I thought, no better from this side. But nobody minds. Nobody cares. Pathetic, that's what it is." The person on the Path of Perfection will look at themselves in a whole new light. As a person now on the Path of Perfection, the path to Gaining Lightness, you'll see the image of your ideal self each and every time you look in the mirror.

As you progress along the core values grid, you may find it quite easy to practice forgiveness. The benefits can be three-fold. First, you'll be able to give up the excuses you used to have to support your faulty eating patterns and sedentary behaviors. Second, you'll be able to heal any resentment or anger you may have accumulated. And third, you will begin practicing the valuable art of "letting go" of those thoughts and things that no longer serve you.

I'm reminded of a story I once heard in which two monks are walking through the woods when they came upon a river they needed to cross. There was a young woman there who wanted to cross the river, but was afraid. The older monk picked up the woman, carried her across the river and put her down safely on the other side. After walking for a while, the younger monk said in a disturbed tone "How is it that you carried that woman across the river. You know that we are to have no physical contact with women." The older monk said "I let the woman go as soon as I set her down. How long will you carry her?" Which begs the question, how long will you carry those things which no longer serve you? Begin to love yourself unconditionally continuing on the path of perfection, the path to Gaining Lightness and give yourself a fulfilling life of health, fitness and happiness.

AFFIRMATIONS RELATED TO THE HEART CHAKRA ARE:

I am worthy of unconditional love.

My self worth is independent of others' opinions.

I love and approve of myself and am at peace with my own feelings.

I forgive myself and others, release the past and move forward with love in my heart.

I open my heart to unconditional love for myself and others.

I easily cut through the cords that bind me.

BEFORE LISTENING TO THE SESSION 5 CD, CHECK IN AND RECORD YOUR CURRENT STATE OF HEALTH:

My current weight is _____ pounds.

I have been successful at Gaining Lightness by letting go of _____ total pounds!

As of this writing, this is how I feel:

Physically:

Mentally:

Emotionally:

Spiritually:

CHAKRA 5 - THROAT

BLUE

The throat chakra is about communication and self expression of thoughts, ideas, wants, needs and feelings. All throughout this book I've made references to negative self-talk. This might include, but may not be limited to, comments to yourself like: "I'm not good enough," "Nothing ever works for me," "I can't do anything right," "I have to swallow my words so as not to offend anyone," "I'm too old to change now." You get the concept, right? Now it's not enough to talk about negative self-talk, it's time to do something about it. You've heard that the past is the past and you can't do anything about it. Well, I'm going to tell you that you can change your history regarding those things others have told you and you have told yourself over and over again.

Before we go there, let's take a look at the differences between the conscious and subconscious minds in relation to their perception of words spoken by others and self-talk, i.e. what you think (remember the quote "Feelings are what you get for thinking the way you do"?). Your conscious mind analyzes everything – what you see, hear, touch, smell and taste. It needs to rationalize or find a reason for everything that occurs. The conscious mind holds your short-term memory, and is from where your will power is drawn. It's the judge, jury and executioner (as in making things happen based on its perception of input received).

The subconscious mind is designed to preserve and

protect the body; which it does through your morals and values, and the autonomic (automatic) nervous system. You don't have to think about beating your heart, taking a breath or where your body needs certain hormones and chemicals, it just happens. It also houses long-term memory, habits (perceived as good or bad by the conscious mind), emotions, and your personality. The subconscious mind is easy to access through meditation or induction and because it takes things literally, it is open to suggestions. Unfortunately, being so literal, it is open to suggestions that both facilitate and hinder your efforts in Gaining Lightness.

Did you ever hear anyone (maybe even you) say something like "I want to lose this weight so badly!" At the conscious level you know what you want this to mean, but to the subconscious mind it means that you want your efforts to turn out "so badly" – and of course, they do. Then there you are scratching your head wondering what the heck happened to your extremely good intentions. While you're scratching your head, a good way to look at it is "I'm only scratching the surface of how easy it might be to turn that negative self-talk around to enhance my goals for Gaining Lightness." And, you're probably thinking that in just the next few paragraphs you might find some great ways to do just that.

A great way to change your thinking style is to stop "shoulding" on yourself. Phrases like "I should lose weight," "I should exercise more," or "I should eat less" have a tendency to instill guilt if you don't follow through. Changing that thought pattern to "I could eat less and exercise more because I know it will aid me in Gaining Lightness" will allow you to be guilt-free and may even have a tendency to encourage you to follow through. Even more

70

powerful would be changing those phrases into affirmations; such as "I enjoy eating light healthy meals"; "I joyfully participate in an exercise program that I enjoy on a regular basis"; and "I am Gaining Lightness at a healthy pace for me." Such self-talk supersedes will power as the subconscious mind will win out every time. Like Einstein said, "Imagination (subconscious mind) is more important than knowledge (conscious mind)"; and it is also more important and powerful than will.

As you begin to express your self-talk differently, it may become necessary to change those expressions with those people with whom you come in contact that may attempt to thwart your progress, unintentionally of course. You know the ones. You may be feeling really good about your progress on your path to Gaining Lightness when someone whom you mention it to says "You know diets don't work; they never worked for you before." Ouch, and this person says they're your friend? Think about how that comment might make you feel. And then, think about how that comment might make you feel if you said something like "You're right, diets never did work for me before, but now I'm in it for me. I don't have to lose anything. I'm Gaining the Lightness that I deserve and I feel great." So, you just reinforced what you know is working for you, and at the same time burst the water balloon of negativity and doubt that was thrown at you before it hit you.

This poor soul may have been critical of you because she is projecting her own past failures on to you or she may be jealous of the results you are gaining now. It's hard to even imagine what others are thinking when they make those off-the-wall comments. As well intentioned as the comments may be in the mind of the speaker, if you take them on as negative they may have a tendency to set you back in your goals. "Oh no" you say, "What if they're right? I'm a loser alright. I can't do anything right. So, I may as well stop what I'm doing and just eat everything in sight until I explode – that will show them." The only thing that will show them is that they'll have a big mess to clean up. Nobody likes a loser and that's precisely why this program is called Gaining Lightness. But by now, your goals are in place, you've been progressing nicely and there's no stopping you now.

Well, except maybe your past history that no longer serves you. It's one thing to thank it for giving you the learning you need from it and letting it go, but you can actually change history – at least your perception of it. Think of a time in your recent or distant past when someone said something hurtful to you. (First, remember that no one can cause you to "feel" or "react" in a certain way — your perception makes it so.) Now, as you remember that scenario, imagine that person in a clown outfit (unless you have a clown phobia, then use some other costume or cartoon character) saying what they said to you in a high-pitched squeaky, whiney voice. Does it have the same impact? Or, do you see a fool just saying something foolish? Wow, remember the saying "Sticks and stones may break my bones but names can never hurt me?" Or, "I'm the rubber, you're the glue; what you say bounces off me and sticks on you." Seeing these scenarios in a humorous light can really change the power they carry. You're probably wondering how you ever let those Bozos' comments affect you in the first place.

Another way to approach changing personal history is to think of a memory that still comes to mind from time to time and it leaves you feeling in a way you would rather not.

When you think of this now, do you feel bad? What resources do you have now (courage, humor, awareness, etc.) that would have made it possible for you to have had a much more useful experience in that situation? Think of a time in your life when you experienced a lot of this resource. Take this special resource back into that problem memory and find out what happens with this resource available to you. Watch and listen in your mind as you relive that old memory in a new way. Take your time with it. As you see the emotional impact diminish, do the exercise again until the scenario no longer makes you feel bad.

In the words of Gen. Joseph Stilwell: "Illegitimis non carborundum," i.e. "Don't let the bastards grind you down." Plan ahead what it is that you might say to these naysayers. Open your throat chakra and say what needs to be said. Whether it's to yourself or others, be kind in your words. Always drop down to the heart chakra and speak from your heart, a place of respect and compassion. If you can't confront others in person, imagine they are sitting in a chair across from you and say it. Say it out loud, like they're really in the room with you and notice how light that makes you feel. And then, use affirmations to keep you on your path to perfection; your path to Gaining Lightness.

AFFIRMATIONS APPROPRIATE
TO THE THROAT CHAKRA ARE:

I speak my truth.

I communicate with my inner self to determine how much to eat.

My body is an expression of my inner beauty.

I maintain a healthy body image each and every step along my path to Gaining Lightness.

I allow my higher self to speak through me.

BEFORE LISTENING TO THE SESSION 6 CD, CHECK IN AND RECORD YOUR CURRENT STATE OF HEALTH:

My current weight is _____ pounds.

I have been successful at Gaining Lightness by letting go of _____ total pounds!

As of this writing, this is how I feel:

Physically:

Mentally:

Emotionally:

Spiritually:

SESSION 7:
CHAKRA 6 -
BROW/THIRD EYE

BROWN

The third eye chakra is about seeing within (know thyself) and outward seeing, i.e. projecting the image you desire. Both of these concepts can be accessed during meditation. You can clear out all that is not you, finding your true self, and visualize yourself in a brand new light. The third eye chakra is the energy center where if you can imagine it, you can manifest it in your life.

Imagining isn't play time, it's powerful. In fact imagination actually means "imaging with power." You hold this power in your mind and in your heart. It's been said that the average person uses only about ten percent of their brain power. So, your brain (your mind) contains a wealth of resources that until now while working through this program, you have not tapped. It gives you the resources to manifest anything you desire. Because you're reading this book and following this program, one of your desires is Gaining Lightness. Accessing this power is quite easy. Think about all the references that are made in relation to you manifesting the life you desire. As (you) think in your heart, so shall (you) be; ask and you shall receive; we are what we think; where your mind goes, energy flows; what you put out, you get back. It's the universal law of attraction.

There are whole books written on these topics. You can sit around reading them until you are blue in the face, or until you're as big as a house, but without action nothing will happen. I'm not suggesting that you don't read the books you want to, but think about it. You can't become a great singer by reading a book, you can't become a great painter by reading a book and you can't be an expert in Gaining Lightness by reading a book (except this one of course because it's guiding you into action). What will serve you best is trusting in yourself!

According to Zetan, keeper of "The Book of All Knowledge," in the movie "Circle of Iron," "There is no enlightenment outside of yourself." And in the movie "The Last Dragon," the Master says to the student, "There is one place that you have not yet looked and it is only there that you will find the master (the answers/the power)" as he pokes Bruce Leroy on the third eye. In other words, everything you need to know about you to make the changes you want to make lies within you. That must be what Einstein meant when he said "Imagination (tapping into the true self) is more important than knowledge (what you might find in books)." My all-time favorite book title, by the way is "There are No Secrets."

The concept is so simple, it's ridiculous. Ouch! What was that? It must have been your self doubt hitting me on the side of the head. That self doubt felt like someone was saying, "If it's so easy, why hasn't anything worked for me up until I found this program?" It's because up until now you haven't believed it could. Everything was projected outside of the self. You were probably blaming fast food, your thyroid, heredity or your constitution. Dr. Wayne Dyer says "You'll see it when you believe it." Now is the time to believe in yourself; and yes, now is the time to believe that the universe is excited about manifesting everything you desire, including Gaining Lightness.

And speaking of self doubt, it's probably a good thing that caterpillars don't have mirrors. Do you think that a caterpillar after seeing itself in a mirror (they're really not that pretty – just my opinion) would believe that if it cocooned itself for a while, got in touch with its inner self, and went through a mysterious transformation that it would actually manifest into a beautiful butterfly? Yet, it does. I wonder how easy it might be for you to look into the mirror seeing your beautiful inner self, and truly feel (know) in your heart that once you focus on your clear intention that you can go into a cocoon of meditation and introspection; and through mysterious transformation emerge as that beautiful butterfly, which is you having your ideal body at your ideal level of health.

You've probably heard that by putting a picture of yourself the weigh you are now on the refrigerator is a good way to keep you out of the fridge. Unfortunately, that keeps the negative aspect of you constantly on your mind because it keeps you focused on a body you are no longer happy with. Rather, put a picture of yourself at your ideal weight on the refrigerator. If you don't have one (a picture of you at your ideal weight, that is), put a picture of someone you want to look like there. You can even put your face on the picture if you'd like. In fact, put these pictures everywhere; on your bedroom mirror, your bathroom mirror and on the dashboard of your car. Doing so will keep you focused on your goal and will constantly remind you to project your ideal image. What you focus your attention on will manifest in your life! What you believe determines how you behave. How you behave determines what you become. What you become determines what your world will become.

"But," you may say, "My belief is that if I project a

picture of my ideal self, exercise, eat in moderation, and do things to reduce stress I will be successful in Gaining Lightness; however how can I act like a thin person if I'm currently not?" Well, I say fake it 'til you make it. Act as if you are already at your ideal weight. This may involve releasing some old beliefs that have the potential to hinder your progress. Here are some beliefs that may need to be blown off:

I need to eat a big breakfast in order to perform better at school/work. Ok, as discussed, it may be in your best interest to eat breakfast to enhance performance, but it's quality, not quantity that is important.

I have to eat everything on my plate. Who says? This belief is fine if you have a plate that is holding a reasonable amount of food. Eating huge quantities of food just because it's on your plate doesn't do you or the rest of the world any good.

I can't eat my favorite foods because I'm on a diet. Remember, your diet is just a new "manner of living" and you can eat anything you want in moderation and still meet your goals. Restriction will cause you to desire the "forbidden fruit" even more.

I just look at food and I gain weight. Yeah, right! If this is the case, you're falling into the "my eyes are bigger than my stomach" thought pattern and you know that it's consuming all that food you're looking at that's been the real problem.

I see food as a reward because my Mom gave me peanut M & Ms whenever I did anything good. Even though your Mom had good intentions and peanut M & Ms are a delicious snack, there are a multitude of other non-food rewards that you can use to satisfy the ego. Use your imagination.

I love chocolate, but it's bad for me. Remember, there are no bad or good foods; your thinking makes it so. Attaching this value judgment to a certain food can cause you undue stress when you eat it. Moderation!!!

People my age always have a difficult time losing weight. People at any age have difficulty losing weight if they hang on to faulty beliefs and have no vision of their true goal. People on the path to Gaining Lightness, such as you, have a much easier time attaining their desired body image.

RATHER, ACCEPT THE NEW BELIEFS FOUND IN THESE THIRD EYE CHAKRA AFFIRMATIONS:

I easily release unwanted beliefs that no longer serve my purpose.

I continually progress toward my ideal body image.

I accept my inner power and resources to effect continual change.

I joyfully release all self doubt and choose a positive way of thinking.

I believe in my heart that with focused intention I easily attain and maintain my ideal weight.

BEFORE LISTENING TO THE SESSION 7 CD, CHECK IN AND RECORD YOUR CURRENT STATE OF HEALTH:

My current weight is _____ pounds.

I have been successful at Gaining Lightness by letting go of _____ total pounds!

As of this writing, this is how I feel:

Physically:

Mentally:

Emotionally:

Spiritually:

SESSION 8:

CHAKRA 7 - CROWN

VIOLET

In the introduction, I described the chakras as vortices of energy. The vortex of chakra 1 opens downward to Mother Earth, the substance of our essence; chakras 2 through 6 open front and back (to the influences of our acquaintances and life experiences); and chakra 7, the crown opens upward to Father Sky. This is the representation of the unified field of consciousness, the field of all possibilities, the divine intelligence, and the source of all manifestation. With the seventh chakra you can draw from the concept of universal life force energy allowing it to flow through the sushumna to all the other energy centers of the body. This energy has many names represented in all religions, as well as the secular realm like: chi, ki, prana, divine spirit, etc.; and regardless of what you call it (I'm sure everyone reading this book has a name for it) it is the energy which guides the creation and functioning of the universe. It is that which you pray to or ask for healing, forgiveness and things. We all have access to this energy in fact, we are this energy.

In the book, "The Zen of Oz," a spiritual view of "The Wizard of Oz," the author writes: "But what the Wizard really gives the Scarecrow, Tin Man and Cowardly Lion is a valuable spiritual lesson, namely that you already possess the attributes that you seek most passionately..." I've also alluded to other convincing references within this book that tell you that you already hold all the power you need to make any change you are passionate about making. The easiest way to tap into the universal life force energy is to quietly go within – getting in touch with your inner nature, your true nature. The most efficient way of doing this is through meditation and contemplation (like using the recorded inductions in this program).

You might ask if meditation or contemplation is important to staying on the path. According to the French philosopher Blaise Pascal, "The sum of a man's problems comes from his inability to be alone in a silent room." The reason such a statement is so critical is that problems can't be resolved at the same level of consciousness where they're formed. Even though habits are held at the subconscious level, they are formed as a result of conscious actions on your part. So, it is absolutely necessary to access the subconscious mind to be the change you want to make. It is certain that you can change your weight. Be the courage. Just be careful if you use mantras in your meditation practice. In the "Guru Guy Guide to the Meaning of Life" Guru Guy suggests: "Yes it is possible to meditate one's way to weight loss and better health! A bit of advice, though: Don't use 'cheesecake' as your mantra."

If you're still doubting the power of the subconscious mind think about the last time you experienced a miracle. I'm not talking about moving mountains with faith the size of a mustard seed, or hearing the voice of the divine coming from a burning bush; but rather something as simple as you having cut your skin and it heals. Science can describe the process by which that happens: You wash the cut to clean it out from bacteria and other matter; cover the cut to protect it from further damage and set up the conditions for healing; platelets come into the area to prevent further bleeding forming a scab; and under that scab a variety of tissues regenerate to heal the wound. The miracle is that you are good as new. Cool! But, what conventional science does not recognize is the universal life force energy that is behind the physical act of healing, although quantum physics makes an admirable attempt. Whether you understand it or not, that energy is there for you whenever you need it and ask for it, consciously or not.

Your subconscious mind is in direct contact with the universal life force energy all the time. It monitors every cell in your body and draws from the "energy" to sustain life. Your subconscious mind is also aware of all of your memories; the functional ones and the ones that up until day one with this program have kept you from attaining your desired weight. Remember the old cartoons and perhaps some other TV shows where a character is trying to decide the best course of action and there's the "devil" image on one shoulder and an "angel" image on the other? One side always seems so fun, yet mischievous and the other side always seems so right.

As you seek the spiritual guidance from the crown chakra to meet your goals such an inner conflict may occur. You will be faced with continual decisions that will test your commitment to yourself – your goals. Some of these decisions may seem trivial like should I drink a cup of coffee with no calories or get a latte which has 180 calories? Should I have dessert just because everyone else at the dinner is having it or should I not? Should I sit on the couch and watch my favorite movie, or exercise while I watch it? Do I get the half sandwich and soup special, or really get my money's worth by having the all you can eat buffet? Watch out for the Yogi Berra dilemma where he says, "You better cut the pizza into 4 pieces because I'm not hungry enough to eat 6."

To always win this battle, sense the questions or the situations at a variety of levels in your body. First, invite the universal life force energy into your crown chakra to attune you to awareness of actions for your highest good. You may then sense the energy in the third eye as intuition or a vision of your goal, and perhaps see how you'll look after attaining your goals. At the throat you may have the experience of expressing your desires, always winning the war of conflicting self-talk. In the heart you will have the inner knowing that it's ok to love yourself enough to make the changes that will keep you at your optimal level of health. As you sense the energy in your solar plexus you continue to take control over your cravings and the actual foods you eat, as well as taking charge of your time and making exercise a priority. In the navel area you may get that gut feeling that some change needs to occur remembering the new relationship you have developed with yourself and the commitments you've made. Or you may sense the energy all the way down to the root chakra where you are now firmly grounded in your desire for change. Wherever you feel the conflict, use the crown chakra to invite the energy of change to flow through you and then you can enjoy watching as "shift happens."

All you have to do is get in touch with the crown chakra to experience the shift you want. But, you'll have to quiet your mind in order to hear the divine guidance you will undoubtedly receive. A quote I found on thinkexist.com says it best: "A wise old owl sat on an oak; the more he saw the less he spoke, the less he spoke, the more he heard; why aren't we like that wise old bird?" The only way to get in touch with that still small voice inside your head is to be still and quiet yourself – then, the more you will hear. The key is to pay attention to what is important to keep you on your path to Gaining Lightness.

To take advantage of that still small voice, tap into the crown chakra to invite spiritual guidance; combine that energy with the solar plexus to take control of your life and surrender the ego to the divine self that is limitless and all embracing. Then, you can use this power to encourage the subconscious mind to assist you in attaining any goal you desire. The beauty of this is that the subconscious mind doesn't know the difference between a real or imagined experience. Try this: Imagine you are holding a fresh lemon. Imagine what it looks like with that vibrant yellow color. Notice what it feels like, smooth, yet slightly dimpled with that little nub on the one end. Now imagine you are cutting into it with a knife slicing through the peel, bursting through those little juice pockets. Notice what it's like to hold the lemon slice up to your mouth which is already salivating; and biting into it. Can you taste it – tart, yet somewhat sweet? Can you imagine the juice squirting everywhere and running down your face? Did you notice how your lips puckered as you imagined biting into it? Seems quite real, doesn't it?

Now using this same type of sensual experience, can you imagine your new youthful, healthy, physically fit body at its ideal weight? If you have a picture of yourself at your ideal weight, get it out and look at it. Remember how you felt at that weight – healthy, energetic, comfortable, attractive or perhaps even sexy. If you were never at what you perceive your ideal weight to be, think of someone who has the ideal body that you seek. Now, see yourself at that ideal weight, wearing the clothing that would make you feel best. Imagine how light you feel; how much energy you have; how comfortable you feel in any situation – socially, at your workplace, at the beach or swimming pool. Notice how easy it is for you in this ideal body to desire exercise, to desire eating in moderation and making you the number one priority in your life. As you hold this vision of your ideal self in your mind's eye, ask the divine spirit at the level of the crown chakra to keep you on track in all that you do. Remember, ask and it is given. Requests at this level put you in direct contact with the unified field of consciousness; the field of all possibilities.

Using your imagination is powerful in this regard and can also make it easy to change your perception of past events and attitudes toward situations, other people and yourself. The power of the crown chakra energy transcends time and space. As an adult, or someone who is wiser now, you can change history by viewing past events with new eyes; your new level of analytical skills; and your ability to understand and forgive. I wonder how many different ways your creative mind might surprise and delight you in its use of this concept to enhance all aspects of your life. Have fun testing it out with all types of things.

IN EXPLORING THE POWER OF THE SEVENTH CHAKRA, YOU CAN USE THE FOLLOWING AFFIRMATIONS TO CONTINUE ON YOUR PATH TO GAINING LIGHTNESS.

I willingly accept the divine guidance of the universe.

I continually access the unified field of consciousness to attain my goals.

I am open to divine intervention on my path to Gaining Lightness.

I open myself to the miracles from the power of the universal life force energy.

I continually expand my power of imagination to be the change I seek.

BEFORE LISTENING TO THE SESSION 8 CD, CHECK IN AND RECORD YOUR CURRENT STATE OF HEALTH:

My current weight is _____ pounds.

I have been successful at Gaining Lightness by letting go of _____ total pounds!

As of this writing, this is how I feel:

Physically:

Mentally:

Emotionally:

Spiritually:

GAINING LIGHTNESS
POST SCRIPT

So, now you've come to the end of the program. Congratulations!!! I'm sure it's been an eight week period of ups and downs, hopefully mostly downs when it comes to the weight you were more than willing to let go of at the beginning. And, mostly ups as you liberated yourself from all the faulty notions that you or others imposed on you; and as you began to employ your new "manner of living." If you truly followed the program; were bold enough to go inside and find the true reasons why you had put on the weight in the first place; and used the chapter information and inductions to motivate you, it would not surprise me that you have let go of 16 to 32 pounds of unwanted weight by now – well on your way to Gaining Lightness. Because results will vary from person to person, view any amount of lightness you've gained as success.

This is just the beginning! You can use the concepts in this book to continue on your path to Gaining Lightness, and as a motivational aid once you've achieved your goal. By identifying the triggers that caused your weight gain initially and the energy centers they are associated with, you now have the resources to maintain that healthy lifestyle you desired and will never have to face the issue of overweightness again.

I applaud you for taking on this endeavor and wish you continued success (as you've had with the Gaining Lightness program) in every aspect of your life.

APPENDIX

Following are the meditations/inductions relating to all the sessions in this book. They are included here in case you feel that by recording and hearing the meditations/inductions in your own voice they would be more effective.

SESSION 1:

GENERAL CONCEPTS MEDITATION/INDUCTION

Find a comfortable position, either sitting or lying down, and when you are ready take a few deep abdominal breaths, engaging your diaphragm muscle between your chest and abdominal cavities. Now begin to focus on your breathing. Notice when you're breathing in; notice when you're breathing out. (Pause) Wherever you are, you may hear a variety of sounds like voices, traffic, air conditioning units or other sounds. Let any outside noises be a reminder to return to focusing on your breath. Breathe in (Pause) and let it go. The conscious mind likes to think — that's what it does. So allow thoughts to drift in, float through, and drift out, letting them be a reminder to come back to your breathing. Notice when you're breathing in; notice when you're breathing out. Just let your conscious mind relax while your subconscious mind is surprised and delighted with the stories or metaphors you are about to hear. As your mind begins to relax, close your eyes and notice how it feels to just be.

Then, notice how it feels to be sitting or lying where you are. Which parts of your body are touching the chair, bed or floor; and which parts are not? Does that place where you're sitting or lying feel soft, or hard? What does the air feel like around your body? Is it warm or cool? What sounds do you hear? Consider just how relaxing those sounds can be. Then, notice the light in the room through your eyelids; just enough light to allow you to see how easy it will be to make all the changes you want to make now.

As you return to focusing on your breath, feeling the breath going deeper and deeper into your body, become aware of your head and face. Allow those muscles to relax; and relax even more with each exhalation. (Pause) Bring your awareness to your neck and shoulders. With each breath, imagine your breath, the universal life force energy, flowing from your neck, across your shoulders, down through your arms, through your hands, and out of your body. Relaxing; releasing all tension. (Pause) Breathe into your chest and upper back, relaxing all those muscles. Then imagine breathing into your abdominal area and mid to low back. As you inhale, allow your abdomen to expand. As you breathe out, exhale fully tightening the abdominal muscles. It's like trying to make your navel touch your spine. (Pause) Imagine breathing the energy into your hips and allowing the energy to flow down through your legs, through your feet and out of your body. Relaxing; releasing all tension.

As your body becomes even more relaxed with each breath, begin to focus on your energy centers. First, at chakra number seven, at the top of your head. You may see the energy as color – seeing violet as the energy swirls. (Pause)

Let the energy flow to six between the eyebrows. You don't even have to think of the color indigo here to feel the effect. (Pause) Bring the energy, your breath down to five at the throat; allowing the color blue to fill this space; noticing your body relaxing even more. (Pause) Let the energy flow to four at your heart center. Be filled with the color green as you relax even deeper. With each breath, you can go deeper and deeper into relaxation; going just to the right level of relaxation to make all the changes you want to make. (Pause) And, the breath goes even deeper to three at your solar plexus. As you think of the color yellow, allow your body to let go and just be. (Pause) You can let that swirling energy flow all the way down to two, at your navel; let the color orange calm your abdominal area. Relaxing; releasing all tension. (Pause) Now, allow your breath to flow through your head, neck, chest, and abdomen and go all the way down to one, at the base of your spine where you may imagine the color red relaxing that area of your body. (Pause)

As your body relaxes, so does your mind. When your conscious mind is relaxed, you access the subconscious mind that holds the wisdom and resources to make all the changes you want to make. In this state, you can look at all aspects of your life objectively, without judgment, and begin to release any bondage you may have had to any actions, thoughts or emotions that are not in alignment with your goals. Just be with these calming, relaxing feelings for a moment or so. (Pause) Your body, mind and spirit are calm, relaxed and ready to be aware of those things that may be distracting you from perfect health and wellness. And ready to become aware of those things that will move you toward your goal.

Now that you are in touch with your subconscious, more

spiritual self, you can begin to think about those things that may or may not be working for you at all levels of your energy system.

Breathing in deeply, focus again on the crown chakra at the top of your head. What is your conceptualization of divine spirit? And, do you feel connected to that unified field of spirit, that field of all possibilities? (Pause) Bringing your awareness to chakra number six between the eyebrows, you might consider whether you have a vision, a dream for how you want your life to be. Do you have goals that will drive you to truly live your passion? (Pause) Relaxing down to five at the throat, you may want to think about how easy it is for you to express yourself, or how easy it might be to communicate what it is you want or need to bring happiness and contentment into your life? (Pause) Now focus deeper into your heart center, four. As you do, imagine the concept of unconditional love. Can you love yourself unconditionally, without judgment for any aspect of your life – body, mind or spirit? You might consider how it feels to be unconditionally loved by yourself or by others? (Pause)

As you breathe in deeply, bring your attention to three at the solar plexus, focus on any control issues you might have; such as, how much control do you have in your job, with your family, with food, or in other aspects of your life? (Pause) Are your emotions in check; in control? (Pause) As you bring your awareness to chakra two, think about your relationships with your family, co-workers, friends and most importantly, yourself. (Pause) Finally, bring your awareness to chakra number one – safety, security issues. How secure are you in your job, your relationships and in other aspects of your life. All you have to do is notice. Don't worry about making any changes at this time – change will occur easily and effortlessly as you need it to. (Pause)

As you allow each breath to take you deeper and deeper into relaxation, imagine you are walking on a path in a quiet, serene place. It might be a meadow with beautiful flowers and plants; or it might be a wooded area with a babbling brook nearby. Notice the colors, bright vibrant colors; relaxing colors. (Pause) Then, listen to the sounds of nature as you are walking along. There might be birds chirping or crickets making that little sound they make; they all seem so calming, so peaceful as your mind relaxes even more. (Pause) Become aware of any fragrances associated with that place; pleasant fragrances; breathe them in; breathe them out; you find them mesmerizing as they allow you to relax even more deeply. Notice the peaceful, relaxing feelings you can experience; now; in this beautiful environment.

While you are walking along the path, the right path; the path to Gaining Lightness, enjoying the sights; the sounds; the fragrances; and the feelings, imagine you are carrying a knapsack, a backpack on your back. It feels heavy because it is the burden that you have been carrying up until now. It's the burden of negativity; things that have been weighing you down; negative self image; negative emotions; faulty eating patterns; poor exercise habits. As you're walking along you have the realization that if you can let these things go, your load will lighten; you recognize it as the lighter weigh. You may remember how that lightness felt in the past; or, you may just imagine it now. (Pause)

Stopping in a beautiful relaxing place along your path, you reach into the backpack and pull out the package that says negative self image. You know you can discard all of those negative concepts; and you know what they were, don't you? (Pause) And, replace them with the attitude that you are good enough; you are deserving of a healthy, fit and trim body; you are confident in who you are. As you walk along the path, you notice that the load is getting lighter, so you decide to let go of more of the burden. Reaching again into the backpack, you pull out the package that says negative emotions. Notice how in your relaxed, calm state that you can discard all of the negative emotions; and you know what they were. (Pause) Replace them with joy, happiness, self love and respect.

Continuing to walk on the path, the right path, you notice that the burden gets lighter and it encourages you to step in the right direction letting go of faulty eating patterns. Reaching into the backpack you remove the package that says faulty eating patterns; looking inside to remember what they were. (Pause) And now realizing that you can discard them and replace them with lighter concepts like eating smaller meals; drinking a full glass of water before meals to give you the sense of fullness; chewing your food slowly to taste each bite and swallowing it before taking the next bite; choosing healthful snacks like fresh fruits and veggies.

As you enjoy the exercise you are getting on the path to Gaining Lightness, you can stop again to pull out the package that says poor exercise habits, and again looking inside to remember what they were. (Pause) Knowing what wasn't working for you makes it easy to replace those heavy faulty habits with lighter ones like setting aside 15 minutes to an hour everyday to engage in some sort of physical activity; easy ones like parking farther from store entrances, or the office and walking a little bit farther; and remembering the concept that your body is designed to move; and it feels good to stretch and build healthy, tone muscle tissue.

As you put on the backpack and continue on your path,

notice how much lighter it feels to be carrying the ideas that support a revitalized, new healthy you. Notice that the path to Gaining Lightness brings you right back here and now to who you really are; what you really are; a vital, healthy human being that deserves to look good; feel good and enjoy each and every day of living with healthy eating and exercise habits that create a fit and trim new you. Start to believe in yourself as you hear the affirmations: "I am at my ideal weight". "I enjoy the perfect kinds and quantities of food to attain and maintain my ideal weight". "I keep my emotions and attitude about health in check."

While your body, mind and spirit integrate those positive aspects of being and becoming more in line with your goals, become aware again of your root chakra 1 at the base of the spine allowing yourself to be secure in your decision to change; moving up to chakra 2 at the navel, feel the joy of establishing a new relationship with you – one of health and well-being. As you become aware of chakra 3 at the solar plexus you might be able to feel the control of being in charge of your life especially as it relates to Gaining Lightness. At chakra 4 at the heart, you may feel a sense of unconditional love for yourself, letting go of any negative thought patterns that up until now have held you back from your goals.

As you move up to chakra 5 at the throat, you may feel a revitalized sense of expression, one that allows you to speak your mind tactfully when others, intentionally or not, try to steer you from your path. In chakra 6, using the concept of a third eye, it might be easy for you now to create a vision of your ideal self, at your ideal weight and level of health. (Pause) As you become aware of the crown chakra at the top of your head, you can reconnect to all that is you. This is your connection with the field of all possibilities. Recognize that your goals will be achieved successfully as you connect with this divine energy and accept your role as a divine being. Ask, and it is given.

Celebrate your divinity as you begin to bring your awareness back into the room. Notice how it feels to be sitting or lying where you are; notice as sounds around you drift into your awareness; notice the light in the room through your eyelids; just enough light to allow you to see how easy it is to make all the changes you want to make now. Begin to move fingers and toes. When you see the number seven representing the crown chakra appear in your mind's eye in the next fifteen or twenty seconds, you can just drift off to sleep, not paying any attention to the rest of this session; or, if you need to be awake, you will come back fully alert, fully refreshed and fully energized.

ROOT CHAKRA
MEDITATION/INDUCTION

Find a comfortable position, either sitting or lying down, and when you are ready take a few deep abdominal breaths, engaging your diaphragm muscle between your chest and abdominal cavities. Now begin to focus on your breathing. Notice when you're breathing in; notice when you're breathing out. (Pause) Wherever you are, you may hear a variety of sounds like voices, traffic, air conditioning units or other sounds. Let any outside noises be a reminder to return to focusing on your breath. Breathe in (Pause) and let it go. The conscious mind likes to think — that's what it does. So allow thoughts to drift in, float through, and drift out, letting them be a reminder to come back to your breathing. Notice when you're breathing in; notice when you're breathing out. Just let your conscious mind relax while your subconscious mind is surprised and delighted with the stories or metaphors you are about to hear. As your mind begins to relax, close your eyes and notice how it feels to just be.

Then, notice how it feels to be sitting or lying where you are. Which parts of your body are touching the chair, bed or floor; and which parts are not? Does that place where you're sitting or lying feel soft, or hard? What does the air feel like around your body? Is it warm or cool? What sounds do you hear? Consider just how relaxing those sounds can be. Then, notice the light in the room through your eyelids; just enough light to allow you to see how easy it will be to make all the changes you want to make now.

As you return to focusing on your breath, feeling the breath going deeper and deeper into your body, become aware of your head and face. Allow those muscles to relax; and relax even more with each exhalation. (Pause) Bring your awareness to your neck and shoulders. With each breath, imagine your breath, the universal life force energy, flowing from your neck, across your shoulders, down through your arms, through your hands, and out of your body. Relaxing; releasing all tension. (Pause) Breathe into your chest and upper back, relaxing all those muscles. Then imagine breathing into your abdominal area and mid to low back. As you inhale, allow your abdomen to expand. As you breathe out, exhale fully tightening the abdominal muscles. It's like trying to make your navel touch your spine. (Pause) Imagine breathing the energy into your hips and allowing the energy to flow down through your legs, through your feet and out of your body. Relaxing; releasing all tension.

As your body becomes even more relaxed with each breath, begin to focus on your energy centers. First, at chakra number seven, at the top of your head. You may see the energy as color – seeing violet as the energy swirls. (Pause) Let the energy flow to six between the eyebrows. You don't even have to think of the color indigo here to feel the effect. (Pause) Bring the energy, your breath down to five at the throat; allowing the color blue to fill this space; noticing your body relaxing even more. (Pause) Let the energy flow to four at your heart center. Be filled with the color green as you relax even deeper. With each breath, you can go deeper and deeper into relaxation; going just to the right level of relaxation to make all the changes you want to make. (Pause) And, the breath goes even deeper to three at your solar plexus. As you think of the color yellow, allow your body to

let go and just be. (Pause) You can let that swirling energy flow all the way down to two, at your navel; let the color orange calm your abdominal area. Relaxing; releasing all tension. (Pause) Now, allow your breath to flow through your head, neck, chest, and abdomen and go all the way down to one, at the base of your spine where you may imagine the color red relaxing that area of your body. (Pause)

As your body relaxes, so does your mind. When your conscious mind is relaxed, you access the subconscious mind that holds the wisdom and resources to make all the changes you want to make. In this state, you can look at all aspects of your life objectively, without judgment, and begin to release any bondage you may have had to any actions, thoughts or emotions that are not in alignment with your goals. Just be with these calming, relaxing feelings for a moment or so. (Pause) Your body, mind and spirit are calm, relaxed and ready to be aware of those things that may be distracting you from perfect health and wellness. And ready to become aware of those things that will move you toward your goal.

As you relax deeper and deeper with each breath, imagine you are in a quiet peaceful place. And in that place, you might be able to picture in your mind's eye a beautiful garden. In that garden are all of your favorite plants and flowers. It might be easy for you to let the beautiful plants and flowers represent all the things about Gaining Lightness that you know to be true: One might represent healthful eating habits like eating small quantities of food, or eating only until you are satisfied physically. Another might reflect how you will develop a sensible exercise program that allows you to joyfully burn off excess calories; and, there may be a beautiful plant or flower that represents stress management and helps you to remember to breathe deeply and slowly, and reminds you to let go of negative thought patterns that do not serve your goals – you know what these are: breathing, releasing, relaxing deeper and deeper into this garden.

Like all plants and flowers, you too have a root system. It is here in the root chakra that you can see the root cause of your weight issues. Only you know what that root cause is, but in this chakra as you sense the feelings of safety and security the issues surrounding the cause may begin to rise to the surface. These issues are like the weeds in the garden that grow unchecked and begin to choke the life out of the beautiful plants and flowers that represent those parts of you that want to change for the better; now. The weeds too have roots that may have woven themselves deeply into your thoughts and actions. To allow yourself to release those negative thought patterns, you need to pull out those weeds by the roots and toss them into a pile. Some of these weeds may have been growing inside for a long time, so you may have to really dig deep, deep inside if you want them gone for good.

It might be fun to give those weeds a name as you identify them. Names like: "always clean your plate," "get your money's worth at a buffet," "stuff down your emotions," "money doesn't grow on trees." Take a moment to think of some others that may have been keeping you from meeting your goals. (Pause)

As you attach a name or phrase to the weeds, imagine yanking them out of the ground; thank them for the purpose they have served (dysfunctional as it is) and toss them into a pile.

The red of the root chakra can represent a fire, a burning desire to release all these negative thought patterns. As you look at the pile of weeds that you are now willing to release, imagine using the fire of the root chakra to burn the weeds, transforming them into the ash that will serve as fertilizer for the plants and flowers that represent your good qualities; those things that are supportive of your goals and allow you to bloom into a new picture of overall health and well-being.

When you have pulled all the weeds and transformed them, all that is left are the beautiful plants and flowers that are the essence of you: confident; worthy of love; successful, at your ideal weight and your ideal level of health. It's your choice whether to nurture the flowers or the weeds. If your garden of attitudes and beliefs are left unchecked, the weeds may flourish on their own and the flowers could be choked out. But now that you've done the weeding you have lots of fertilized soil with which to create and nurture a new pattern of growth. This new, healthy growth will require steady, regular attention on your goals.

You may find it inspiring at this time to remember aspects of the commitments that were made as a result of beginning this journey toward Gaining Lightness. You committed to honor you just because you are you. You continue to forgive yourself and others for whatever it is you need to release. You let go of emotions and feelings which no longer serve you and you naturally let go of the weight that has accumulated as a result. You pattern your eating habits in such a way that you are Gaining Lightness by 2 to 4 pounds per week until you reach your ideal weight. You engage in some form of exercise that is pleasing to you at least 3 times per week. And, you have a clear picture of the ideal you; at your ideal weight.

Now that you are free of the negative thought patterns that were at the root cause of your weight issues, it may be easy to visualize yourself in that beautiful garden at your ideal weight and level of health. Notice how it feels to picture yourself being successful at Gaining Lightness. Look ahead at that time when you have gained the lightness you desire. You may be wearing an outfit that makes you feel really good; or, you may be doing an activity that up until now you were unable to do. (Pause) And now consider how easy it might be for you to imagine a loved one, someone who really cares about you and loves you coming into the garden with you. Can you imagine what that person might say to you knowing that you've achieved your goals; you are successful at Gaining Lightness; and you are completely happy with the new you? (Pause) Notice how it feels to hear those supportive words. (Pause)

As you allow yourself to breathe in and internalize those loving, caring words, allow yourself to become aware of your body in your current surroundings and notice the calmness and relaxation you are experiencing. Notice how good it feels to be in the process of Gaining Lightness. You may from time to time remember the garden and how important it is to nurture it; nurture you as you provide nourishment for the physical body, continually weeding the garden from those negative thought patterns, freeing your mind and emotions; and allowing for the spiritual growth from within which will guide you to change anything you need to change to support your goals. Listen to these affirmations that will help to support your goals: "I am secure in my life as it is"; "My work life is filled with abundance and prosperity"; "I know that I always have enough to eat to sustain life and healthful living"; "I develop and maintain relationships that support my physical, mental/emotional and spiritual well-being"; "I am secure and grounded in this physical form".

While your body, mind and spirit integrate those positive aspects of being and becoming more in line with your goals, become aware again of your root chakra 1 at the base of the spine allowing yourself to be secure in your decision to change; moving up to chakra 2 at the navel, feel the joy of establishing a new relationship with you – one of health and well-being. As you become aware of chakra 3 at the solar plexus you might be able to feel the control of being in charge of your life especially as it relates to Gaining Lightness. At chakra 4 at the heart, you may feel a sense of unconditional love for yourself, letting go of any negative thought patterns that up until now have held you back from your goals.

As you move up to chakra 5 at the throat, you may feel a revitalized sense of expression, one that allows you to speak your mind tactfully when others, intentionally or not, try to steer you from your path. In chakra 6, using the concept of a third eye, it might be easy for you now to create a vision of your ideal self, at your ideal weight and level of health. (Pause) As you become aware of the crown chakra at the top of your head, you can reconnect to all that is you. This is your connection with the field of all possibilities. Recognize that your goals will be achieved successfully as you connect with this divine energy and accept your role as a divine being. Ask, and it is given.

Celebrate your divinity as you begin to bring your awareness back into the room. Notice how it feels to be sitting or lying where you are; notice as sounds around you drift into your awareness; notice the light in the room through your eyelids; just enough light to allow you to see how easy it is to make all the changes you want to make now. Begin to move fingers and toes. When you see the number seven representing the crown chakra appear in your mind's eye in the next fifteen or twenty seconds, you can just drift off to sleep, not paying any attention to the rest of this session; or, if you need to be awake, you will come back fully alert, fully refreshed and fully energized.

SESSION 3:

NAVEL CHAKRA MEDITATION/INDUCTION

Find a comfortable position, either sitting or lying down, and when you are ready take a few deep abdominal breaths, engaging your diaphragm muscle between your chest and abdominal cavities. Now begin to focus on your breathing. Notice when you're breathing in; notice when you're breathing out. (Pause) Wherever you are, you may hear a variety of sounds like voices, traffic, air conditioning units or other sounds. Let any outside noises be a reminder to return to focusing on your breath. Breathe in (Pause) and let it go. The conscious mind likes to think — that's what it does. So allow thoughts to drift in, float through, and drift out, letting them be a reminder to come back to your breathing. Notice when you're breathing in; notice when you're breathing out. Just let your conscious mind relax while your subconscious mind is surprised and delighted with the stories or metaphors you are about to hear. As your mind begins to relax, close your eyes and notice how it feels to just be.

Then, notice how it feels to be sitting or lying where you are. Which parts of your body are touching the chair, bed or floor; and which parts are not? Does that place where you're sitting or lying feel soft, or hard? What does the air feel like around your body? Is it warm or cool? What sounds do you hear? Consider just how relaxing those sounds can be. Then, notice the light in the room through your eyelids; just enough light to allow you to see how easy it will be to make all the changes you want to make now.

As you return to focusing on your breath, feeling the breath going deeper and deeper into your body, become aware of your head and face. Allow those muscles to relax; and relax even more with each exhalation. (Pause) Bring your awareness to your neck and shoulders. With each breath, imagine your breath, the universal life force energy, flowing from your neck, across your shoulders, down through your arms, through your hands, and out of your body. Relaxing; releasing all tension. (Pause) Breathe into your chest and upper back, relaxing all those muscles. Then imagine breathing into your abdominal area and mid to low back. As you inhale, allow your abdomen to expand. As you breathe out, exhale fully tightening the abdominal muscles. It's like trying to make your navel touch your spine. (Pause) Imagine breathing the energy into your hips and allowing the energy to flow down through your legs, through your feet and out of your body. Relaxing; releasing all tension.

As your body becomes even more relaxed with each breath, begin to focus on your energy centers. First, at chakra number seven, at the top of your head. You may see the energy as color – seeing violet as the energy swirls. (Pause) Let the energy flow to six between the eyebrows. You don't even have to think of the color indigo here to feel the effect. (Pause) Bring the energy, your breath down to five at the throat; allowing the color blue to fill this space; noticing your body relaxing even more. (Pause) Let the energy flow to four at your heart center. Be filled with the color green as you relax even deeper. With each breath, you can go deeper and deeper into relaxation; going just to the right level of relaxation to make all the changes you want to make. (Pause) And, the breath goes even deeper to three at your solar plexus. As you think of the color yellow, allow your body to

let go and just be. (Pause) You can let that swirling energy flow all the way down to two, at your navel; let the color orange calm your abdominal area. Relaxing; releasing all tension. (Pause) Now, allow your breath to flow through your head, neck, chest, and abdomen and go all the way down to one, at the base of your spine where you may imagine the color red relaxing that area of your body. (Pause)

As your body relaxes, so does your mind. When your conscious mind is relaxed, you access the subconscious mind that holds the wisdom and resources to make all the changes you want to make. In this state, you can look at all aspects of your life objectively, without judgment, and begin to release any bondage you may have had to any actions, thoughts or emotions that are not in alignment with your goals. Just be with these calming, relaxing feelings for a moment or so. (Pause) Your body, mind and spirit are calm, relaxed and ready to be aware of those things that may be distracting you from perfect health and wellness. And ready to become aware of those things that will move you toward your goal.

As you allow each breath to take you deeper and deeper into relaxation, imagine you are walking on a path in a quiet, serene place. It might be a meadow with beautiful flowers and plants; or it might be a wooded area with a babbling brook nearby. Notice the colors, bright vibrant colors; relaxing colors. Then, listen to the sounds of nature as you are walking along. There might be birds chirping or crickets making that little sound they make. They all seem so calming, so peaceful as your mind relaxes even more. Become aware of any fragrances associated with that place; pleasant fragrances. Breathe them in; breathe them out. You find them mesmerizing as they allow you to relax even more deeply. Notice the peaceful, relaxing feelings you can experience; now; in this beautiful environment. (Pause)

While you are walking along the path enjoying the sights; the sounds; the fragrances; and the feelings, imagine you come to a fork in the road. One road leads to the right. It's the right path which has a sign that says "Gaining Lightness"; and the other leads to the left with a sign that says "Your current weight and state of health – or worse!" You know which one to pick, but for now, take a few steps down the path to the left. This is the path you've been on up until now. And, along that path you have encountered many relationships with other people; with food; with exercise; and with yourself.

Many of those relationships have been pleasant and valuable for your quality of life; while others have been destructive in relation to your goals and state of health and well-being. In fact, they may have been loaded with emotions. You may have had loved ones unknowingly leading you down this path of destruction by telling you to "clean your plate", even though they filled your plate with enough food for 2 people; or laying on the emotional guilt of people starving in other countries because you didn't finish all your food; or, eat all your food so you can grow up BIG. You may have mistakenly filled the emotional emptiness you felt with food when what you really wanted was companionship and touch, either nurturing or intimate.

You may have used food for entertainment or socializing, using meals or gatherings as a way to draw family, friends or co-workers together. You may even remember a time when you held onto food or drink at a gathering, or stayed close to the table of food as a comfort measure to avoid having to communicate with others due to insecurities. As you are

Gaining Lightness, you are becoming more confident and self-assured.

Your past attitude about exercise may have had the emotional component of a gym teacher or classmates making fun of you, or always being picked last in team events, or being pushed into a sport you didn't want to participate in by your parents, turning you off to all types of physical activity. And finally, with all this emotional baggage you've been carrying around, your relationship with yourself has suffered. Perhaps you began to crave the loving attention that you deserve creating an emotional void or emptiness. As you think back on the emotional situations you've been in over the years try to look at them objectively and without judgment. (Pause) It's time to thank those old emotions and feelings for being there when you needed them; and release them now because it's now time to move on.

In the past, you may have found yourself on the wrong path, the one with many ruts along the way, falling into feelings of helplessness and hopelessness. Having fallen into those ruts and having experienced those habits over and over again there comes a time when you now become aware, you realize your past mistakes and you find it easy to get out. Finally, you realize there is another way, the right way and you can walk down another path. It's time for you now to walk down that other path; the right path; the path to "Gaining Lightness". Start down that path, the right path; now.

As you do, first, see your relationship with yourself changing. What would that ideal relationship with yourself look like? (Pause) Do you give yourself all the love you deserve? Do you easily let go of old patterns of negative self-talk? You find it easy to give yourself compliments and admiration. You joyfully build yourself up, offering yourself support as you would do for a close companion, a friend or a child.

Think about all those things you might do differently to enjoy a new relationship with yourself; things that would direct your thoughts to "know thyself". They might be things like taking time to meditate and contemplate; setting aside time for pampering like taking a warm bath surrounded by aromatherapy; spending time in nature, perhaps stretched out on a hammock or lying in the grass watching the clouds move and change; catching up on the books you want to read; doing crafts like needlework, drawing or writing. (Pause)

Continue the new relationship with you by forgiving; forgetting; changing into a pattern of self-love and self-respect. The keys to a great relationship are commitment, communication and responsibility. The commitment you made to yourself when starting Gaining Lightness is one of self-love and self-respect; letting go of emotions and feelings which no longer serve you; letting go of the excess weight that has accumulated; keeping your mental and physical health a priority in your life; and continuing to look forward to many more years of fun, fitness, health and happiness.

Then you can begin communicating with yourself to change your relationship with food by using positive self-talk about moderation in eating habits. As you progress on the path to Gaining Lightness, you will find it easy to decide whether your hunger is biological or psychological. Then you can decide to satisfy that hunger with food; or with emotional fulfillment, whichever is most appropriate. If you want to feed your body because of a real physical hunger, do it; but do it consciously. Remember though that it takes about 20 minutes for your digestive system to register fullness. So, eat slowly; chew your food consciously so you can enjoy the textures, the flavors and truly enjoy the satisfaction of a good meal; fully swallow each mouthful before taking the next bite. And when you feel full it will be easy to stop eating, even if it means leaving some on the plate or just throwing it away. It's your choice – you can throw it in the trash can, or you can be the trash can.

Choose the right path now. Then, you can change your attitude toward food from "living to eat" to "eating to live"; always in moderation. If the hunger is to fill an emotional void, or an attempt to stuff down your feelings, then feed it with creativity, new ideas, social conversation, opportunities, and exciting challenges for mental or emotional growth and change. If it's a sexual hunger, explore with your mate ways to make intimacy more fulfilling. If you're not currently in relationship, remember the phrase "it takes two to tango" pertains only to dancing.

You can also change your relationship with exercise. Remember, with over 600 muscles, your body is designed to move. Think now about what type of exercise would be fulfilling to you. (Pause) Can you imagine how good your body would feel just by stretching everyday? (Pause) It's time to let go of any negative thought patterns you may have had about exercising. It's time to think about your health; your well-being; and how easy it might be to choose an exercise program that fits your current physical condition. Commit now to giving yourself at least 5 to 30 minutes daily for exercise. You know how easy it would be to give a friend 5 to 30 minutes of your time if they needed your support. Be your own best friend. Give yourself the support; commit; you are worth it. Believe it!

You can enjoy the challenge of changing your relationship with yourself; changing your relationships with others; changing your relationship with food; finding the right exercise plan for you; and knowing when to, and when not to listen to others' opinions about what and how much you should be eating. When pressured by others, "just say no". It's your responsibility – the ability to respond appropriately in personal and social situations. Our uniqueness as human beings is that we have the ability to adapt to change. The changes you want to make are as easy as you want them to be. One step at a time, on the right path, will keep you moving in the right direction; closer to your goals. Each step allows you to grow stronger, leaner, and healthier each and every day. Each step on the right path moves you closer to a newer and better you.

To maintain your focus on the right path, remember the affirmations: "I nourish only those relationships that support my goals"; "I grow emotionally stronger everyday"; "I fill my emotional voids with love"; "I am continually developing healthy relationships"; "I express my sexuality and creativity with joy".

While your body, mind and spirit integrate those positive aspects of being and becoming more in line with your goals, become aware again of your root chakra 1 at the base of the spine allowing yourself to be secure in your decision to change; moving up to chakra 2 at the navel, feel the joy of establishing a new relationship with you – one of health and well-being. As you become aware of chakra 3 at the solar plexus you might be able to feel the control of being in charge of your life especially as it relates to Gaining Lightness. At chakra 4 at the heart, you may feel a sense of unconditional love for yourself, letting go of any negative

thought patterns that up until now have held you back from your goals.

As you move up to chakra 5 at the throat, you may feel a revitalized sense of expression, one that allows you to speak your mind tactfully when others, intentionally or not, try to steer you from your path. In chakra 6, using the concept of a third eye, it might be easy for you now to create a vision of your ideal self, at your ideal weight and level of health. (Pause) As you become aware of the crown chakra at the top of your head, you can reconnect to all that is you. This is your connection with the field of all possibilities. Recognize that your goals will be achieved successfully as you connect with this divine energy and accept your role as a divine being. Ask, and it is given.

Celebrate your divinity as you begin to bring your awareness back into the room. Notice how it feels to be sitting or lying where you are; notice as sounds around you drift into your awareness; notice the light in the room through your eyelids; just enough light to allow you to see how easy it is to make all the changes you want to make now. Begin to move fingers and toes. When you see the number seven representing the crown chakra appear in your mind's eye in the next fifteen or twenty seconds, you can just drift off to sleep, not paying any attention to the rest of this session; or, if you need to be awake, you will come back fully alert, fully refreshed and fully energized.

SESSION 4:

SOLAR PLEXUS CHAKRA MEDITATION/INDUCTION

Find a comfortable position, either sitting or lying down, and when you are ready take a few deep abdominal breaths, engaging your diaphragm muscle between your chest and abdominal cavities. Now begin to focus on your breathing. Notice when you're breathing in; notice when you're breathing out. (Pause) Wherever you are, you may hear a variety of sounds like voices, traffic, air conditioning units or other sounds. Let any outside noises be a reminder to return to focusing on your breath. Breathe in (Pause) and let it go. The conscious mind likes to think — that's what it does. So allow thoughts to drift in, float through, and drift out, letting them be a reminder to come back to your breathing. Notice when you're breathing in; notice when you're breathing out. Just let your conscious mind relax while your subconscious mind is surprised and delighted with the stories or metaphors you are about to hear. As your mind begins to relax, close your eyes and notice how it feels to just be.

Then, notice how it feels to be sitting or lying where you are. Which parts of your body are touching the chair, bed or floor; and which parts are not? Does that place where you're sitting or lying feel soft, or hard? What does the air feel like around your body? Is it warm or cool? What sounds do you hear? Consider just how relaxing those sounds can be. Then, notice the light in the room through your eyelids; just enough light to allow you to see how easy it will be to make all the changes you want to make now.

As you return to focusing on your breath, feeling the breath going deeper and deeper into your body, become aware of your head and face. Allow those muscles to relax; and relax even more with each exhalation. (Pause) Bring your awareness to your neck and shoulders. With each breath, imagine your breath, the universal life force energy, flowing from your neck, across your shoulders, down through your arms, through your hands, and out of your body. Relaxing; releasing all tension. (Pause) Breathe into your chest and upper back, relaxing all those muscles. Then imagine breathing into your abdominal area and mid to low back. As you inhale, allow your abdomen to expand. As you breathe out, exhale fully tightening the abdominal muscles. It's like trying to make your navel touch your spine. (Pause) Imagine breathing the energy into your hips and allowing the energy to flow down through your legs, through your feet and out of your body. Relaxing; releasing all tension.

As your body becomes even more relaxed with each breath, begin to focus on your energy centers. First, at chakra number seven, at the top of your head. You may see the energy as color – seeing violet as the energy swirls. (Pause) Let the energy flow to six between the eyebrows. You don't even have to think of the color indigo here to feel the effect. (Pause) Bring the energy, your breath down to five at the throat; allowing the color blue to fill this space; noticing your body relaxing even more. (Pause) Let the energy flow to four at your heart center. Be filled with the color green as you relax even deeper. With each breath, you can go deeper and deeper into relaxation; going just to the right level of relaxation to make all the changes you want to make. (Pause) And, the breath goes even deeper to three at your solar plexus. As you think of the color yellow, allow your body to

let go and just be. (Pause) You can let that swirling energy flow all the way down to two, at your navel; let the color orange calm your abdominal area. Relaxing; releasing all tension. (Pause) Now, allow your breath to flow through your head, neck, chest, and abdomen and go all the way down to one, at the base of your spine where you may imagine the color red relaxing that area of your body. (Pause)

As your body relaxes, so does your mind. When your conscious mind is relaxed, you access the subconscious mind that holds the wisdom and resources to make all the changes you want to make. In this state, you can look at all aspects of your life objectively, without judgment, and begin to release any bondage you may have had to any actions, thoughts or emotions that are not in alignment with your goals. Just be with these calming, relaxing feelings for a moment or so. (Pause) Your body, mind and spirit are calm, relaxed and ready to be aware of those things that may be distracting you from perfect health and wellness. And ready to become aware of those things that will move you toward your goal.

While your body and mind relax even more with each breath, it might be fun to imagine taking a boat trip in a canal, much like the gondolas on the canals of Venice. Your trip will be down the alimentary canal – your digestive tract, the canal that begins at your mouth and runs continuously through your body. This will be a very safe boat ride because it's controlled totally by your imagination. It's always safe to go inside. If you'd like, you can imagine putting on a safety vest just for security. Then, imagine a boat. It might be long and slender; or, it might be just a tiny bit broader on each end with a trim midline, much like an hour glass shape, with a perfectly round bottom.

Imagine yourself getting into the boat, fully in control and ready to take this journey to a place within you where no one else has ever been; a place of mystery and adventure. The boat is sitting on a waterway that is calm and clear, and the scenery is just as beautiful as you can imagine. As you begin to move forward in the canal, picture a cave ahead and notice a blue light that looks relaxing, calming and inviting. As you enter the cave, the path is clear and bright; much like your future with Gaining Lightness - you know you're on the right path. The water is calm and the walls of the cave are illuminated by colors and shapes that are pleasing, calming and relaxing. Take a deep breath; and as you let it out, let the muscles of your chest and abdomen relax fully. Notice as the walls of the cave turn to a calming, relaxing green. You may have noticed the walls of the cave expand; and contract, making it easy for you to move along in the canal; going deeper and deeper inside.

As you move along, in the distance you see a bright yellow light. It's the light of your solar plexus; the control center for your metabolism, your appetite, your emotions and your activity levels. Entering the control center, you notice that it's safe to stop the boat; get out; and observe what's there. You know that the yellow light means caution, or a time to reflect on your emotions and your eating and exercise habits. As you reflect, you may remember times when you ate so much that it was terribly uncomfortable; perhaps to the point where you found it difficult to breathe. (Pause) You may remember times when you were extremely sedentary and thought that exercise was hopeless; (Pause) times when your muscles were sore from inactivity and it felt uncomfortable to move at all. (Pause) Or you may reflect on emotions that you have stuffed down because it was too hurtful to be aware of them. (Pause) As you look to one side of the control center, notice a control panel. There are switches for appetite, exercise and emotions. You know it's now time to reset those switches putting you in full control of your eating habits, your desire to exercise regularly, your emotions and your life.

Look over and picture the switch for appetite control. Is it in the position of "no limits"; "pack it in so I get my money's worth"; or, "eat what you want, dieting is useless"? You might ask yourself, "What are you allowing to enter your alimentary canal?" Imagine how easy it might be to take in moderate amounts of proteins, carbohydrates and fats. Remember that the stomach is only about the size of a small fist. The amount of food that you take in at one sitting fills only the space of your cupped hands. Imagine how comfortable your body will feel when you eat the right amounts of food. (Pause) You can consider drinking a full glass of water a half hour before meals to set up optimal conditions for digestion. You may consider drinking one to two glasses about 2 hours after your meal to move things gently through the digestive canal. You can adjust the control switch to let you know when you are physically full, when your physical body is satisfied with your caloric intake. In your mind's eye, flip that appetite control switch to "Moderation".

Then, notice the switch for exercise; is it in the position of "none", or "rely on excuses"? Remember your body is designed to move. You can probably recall how good it feels just to stretch a little bit before getting out of bed. Imagine how good your body would feel if you were to get out of bed and stretch and exercise consciously for 5 to 30 minutes everyday. (Pause) Exercise can be as simple as walking, especially in nature where you can enjoy the relaxing sights and sounds. Or, you may enjoy exercising to a video which has a leader and inspiring music. Perhaps you are drawn to join a fitness club with a friend and be motivated by a personal trainer. As you joyfully participate in any of these activities, you will become stronger, leaner, healthier and have more energy to do the things you enjoy doing during the day. In your mind's eye, flip that exercise switch to "every day in moderation".

Bring your awareness to the emotion switch. Is that switch turned to "stuff them down"; "ignore them"; "eat for emotional fulfillment"; or, "out of control". It's ok to experience and acknowledge emotions. They're clues to how you are feeling at any given time. And remember, feelings are what you get for thinking the way you do. Imagine how different it would be to feel your emotions objectively, to notice what really needs to be comforted, allow yourself to breathe deeply, relax your entire body and just be with the feelings; then take appropriate action. You may find yourself assertively telling others what's on your mind. You may find that sometimes it is very cleansing to cry. Or, it might just be fun, when appropriate, to just laugh things off. In your mind's eye, flip that emotion switch to "appropriate expression".

The control center is your center of transformation; transformation of food to energy; transformation of exercise to energy; and transformation of emotions to energy - every thing in moderation. Now that you've made the control center changes you needed to make, allow yourself to get back in the boat, thanking that part of you that puts you in total control and continue moving down the alimentary canal. Notice how clear the water is, how calming and relaxing it is to move on. As you float along, the lighting in the cave turns to orange; and you can think about the new relationship you have with yourself as you transform. Continuing on, you approach a red light in the distance, the end of the cave; and I'm not going to tell you where you're coming out, but elimination is a healthy part of the digestive process. It's the process that reminds you to let go of all the shh-stuff that no longer serves you, like negative self-talk, grudges and faulty misconceptions you may have heard about how to live your life. Allow yourself to take a deep breath bringing your boat safely to the dock.

As you step out of the boat and on to solid ground, the solid ground of commitment, the solid ground of control, remember these affirmations: "I eagerly gain control of all aspects of my life"; "I lovingly accept myself and all the good I am capable of"; "I am free of all negative thought patterns"; "I recognize my personal power and use it to attain my goals".

While your body, mind and spirit integrate those positive aspects of being and becoming more in line with your goals, become aware again of your root chakra 1 at the base of the spine allowing yourself to be secure in your decision to change; moving up to chakra 2 at the navel, feel the joy of establishing a new relationship with you – one of health and well-being. As you become aware of chakra 3 at the solar plexus you might be able to feel the control of being in charge of your life especially as it relates to Gaining Lightness. At chakra 4 at the heart, you may feel a sense of unconditional love for yourself, letting go of any negative thought patterns that up until now have held you back from your goals.

As you move up to chakra 5 at the throat, you may feel a revitalized sense of expression, one that allows you to speak your mind tactfully when others, intentionally or not, try to steer you from your path. In chakra 6, using the concept of a third eye, it might be easy for you now to create a vision of your ideal self, at your ideal weight and level of health. (Pause) As you become aware of the crown chakra at the top of your head, you can reconnect to all that is you. This is your connection with the field of all possibilities. Recognize that your goals will be achieved successfully as you connect with this divine energy and accept your role as a divine being. Ask, and it is given.

Celebrate your divinity as you begin to bring your awareness back into the room. Notice how it feels to be sitting or lying where you are; notice as sounds around you drift into your awareness; notice the light in the room through your eyelids; just enough light to allow you to see how easy it is to make all the changes you want to make now. Begin to move fingers and toes. When you see the number seven representing the crown chakra appear in your mind's eye in the next fifteen or twenty seconds, you can just drift off to sleep, not paying any attention to the rest of this session; or, if you need to be awake, you will come back fully alert, fully refreshed and fully energized.

SESSION 5:
HEART CHAKRA MEDITATION/INDUCTION

Find a comfortable position, either sitting or lying down, and when you are ready take a few deep abdominal breaths, engaging your diaphragm muscle between your chest and abdominal cavities. Now begin to focus on your breathing. Notice when you're breathing in; notice when you're breathing out. (Pause) Wherever you are, you may hear a variety of sounds like voices, traffic, air conditioning units or other sounds. Let any outside noises be a reminder to return to focusing on your breath. Breathe in (Pause) and let it go. The conscious mind likes to think — that's what it does. So allow thoughts to drift in, float through, and drift out, letting them be a reminder to come back to your breathing. Notice when you're breathing in; notice when you're breathing out. Just let your conscious mind relax while your subconscious mind is surprised and delighted with the stories or metaphors you are about to hear. As your mind begins to relax, close your eyes and notice how it feels to just be.

Then, notice how it feels to be sitting or lying where you are. Which parts of your body are touching the chair, bed or floor; and which parts are not? Does that place where you're sitting or lying feel soft, or hard? What does the air feel like around your body? Is it warm or cool? What sounds do you hear? Consider just how relaxing those sounds can be. Then, notice the light in the room through your eyelids; just enough light to allow you to see how easy it will be to make all the changes you want to make now.

As you return to focusing on your breath, feeling the breath going deeper and deeper into your body, become aware of your head and face. Allow those muscles to relax; and relax even more with each exhalation. (Pause) Bring your awareness to your neck and shoulders. With each breath, imagine your breath, the universal life force energy, flowing from your neck, across your shoulders, down through your arms, through your hands, and out of your body. Relaxing; releasing all tension. (Pause) Breathe into your chest and upper back, relaxing all those muscles. Then imagine breathing into your abdominal area and mid to low back. As you inhale, allow your abdomen to expand. As you breathe out, exhale fully tightening the abdominal muscles. It's like trying to make your navel touch your spine. (Pause) Imagine breathing the energy into your hips and allowing the energy to flow down through your legs, through your feet and out of your body. Relaxing; releasing all tension.

As your body becomes even more relaxed with each breath, begin to focus on your energy centers. First, at chakra number seven, at the top of your head. You may see the energy as color – seeing violet as the energy swirls. (Pause) Let the energy flow to six between the eyebrows. You don't even have to think of the color indigo here to feel the effect. (Pause) Bring the energy, your breath down to five at the throat; allowing the color blue to fill this space; noticing your body relaxing even more. (Pause) Let the energy flow to four at your heart center. Be filled with the color green as you relax even deeper. With each breath, you can go deeper and deeper into relaxation; going just to the right level of relaxation to make all the changes you want to make. (Pause) And, the breath goes even deeper to three at your solar plexus. As you think of the color yellow, allow your body to

let go and just be. (Pause) You can let that swirling energy flow all the way down to two, at your navel; let the color orange calm your abdominal area. Relaxing; releasing all tension. (Pause) Now, allow your breath to flow through your head, neck, chest, and abdomen and go all the way down to one, at the base of your spine where you may imagine the color red relaxing that area of your body. (Pause)

As your body relaxes, so does your mind. When your conscious mind is relaxed, you access the subconscious mind that holds the wisdom and resources to make all the changes you want to make. In this state, you can look at all aspects of your life objectively, without judgment, and begin to release any bondage you may have had to any actions, thoughts or emotions that are not in alignment with your goals. Just be with these calming, relaxing feelings for a moment or so. (Pause) Your body, mind and spirit are calm, relaxed and ready to be aware of those things that may be distracting you from perfect health and wellness. And ready to become aware of those things that will move you toward your goal.

That perfect health and wellness can best be attained when body, mind and spirit are filled with the energy of the earth, and of the universal life force. Become aware of your root chakra again. Imagine bringing the energy of mother earth into the root chakra thinking of the nourishment of the food she provides and the lightness you get from the air that you breathe – in - deeply. Allow that sense of fulfillment to move up to the area of the navel and solar plexus where the nutrients of the earth's nourishment are transformed into energy for your body. As the energy moves up in the body, bring it into your heart center.

The heart is an amazing organ that has 2 entry halls, the

right and left atria to receive; and 2 sections for giving, the right and left ventricles. Your life blood brings nourishment to the heart through the right atrium – you might imagine that nourishment being the love you receive from family and friends. But to make it really useful that love needs to be combined with the love of Spirit or God, the Divine associated with the universal life force energy – father sky. So your heart pumps the blood from the right ventricle into the lungs. As you breathe in deeply, imagine breathing in the life force, Spirit, through your crown chakra at the top of your head. This is the unconditional love of that which created you; that which controls the functioning of the automatic systems of your body. Allow the energy of true unconditional love to move into your third eye; you don't even have to think about your ideal body image - now.

Bring the energy through your throat chakra as you breathe deeply, and into your lungs to merge with the nutrients of the earth. As those energies merge, they are pumped into the left atrium of the heart. It is the left ventricle that pumps all that love—from family; from friends; from the universal life force of Spirit—throughout your entire being.

As you imagine all of the energy of unconditional love converging in your heart, all of the stress in the heart chakra can be released through forgiveness. Think of those people, including yourself, and situations that you feel may have played a role in your eating habits that no longer serve you. (Pause) An easy way for you to release the blame or guilt attached is to imagine—one at a time—those people, including yourself, and situations having an attachment to your heart chakra. Each person or situation may have a cord connecting them to your heart. Even though you may still have great love for these people regardless of the situations they may have put you in, you can forgive them; thereby cutting the cord that holds any negativity; while at the same time maintaining an appropriate attachment to their friendship and love. It may be overwhelming if there are a lot of people or situations that need to be addressed, but even by cutting one cord, you are on your way to Gaining Lightness. It will be interesting to notice how much lighter you feel with every cord you cut. You may also notice how happy it makes you feel to forgive yourself and others. You, not events, have the power to make you happy or unhappy today. You can choose. Which will it be.

Take your time. Notice the attachment each cord has to your heart. You may even want to imagine using a giant pair of scissors to cut all the cords that you are willing to cut now. Forgiving; releasing the power of negativity. (Pause)

There may also be certain foods or snacks that you have had an attachment to which may not be contributing to your goals. As you think of each of these foods or snacks, imagine that cord of attachment. By focusing on your goals for Gaining Lightness it may become easy for you to cut the cords. As you do, thank that food or snack for being there when you needed it; then release any attachment you may have had to it. (Pause) Any future choice to eat these foods becomes a conscious one. And you know that moderation is in your best interest.

As you cut each cord, you will find it easier and easier to forgive and let go. This is key in the Path of Perfection. It's time to give up the excuses you used to have to support past eating, and sedentary behaviors; you can heal any resentment or anger you may have accumulated; and you are practicing the valuable art of letting go of those thoughts and things that no longer serve you. It's OK to tell yourself "I Love You" and mean it.

As you allow yourself to breathe in and internalize those loving, caring words, allow yourself to become aware of your body in your current surroundings and notice the calmness and relaxation you are experiencing; notice how good it feels to be in the process of Gaining Lightness. You may from time to time remember the four chambers of the heart and how they relate to giving and receiving. It's Ok to accept love from others and yourself. It's kind of interesting how the heart is that place which is important for both nutritional and spiritual nourishment. It is important to nurture it; nurture you as you provide nourishment for the physical body, the mind and the spirit, continually cutting the cords from those negative thought patterns freeing your mind and emotions and allowing for the spiritual growth from within which will guide you to change anything you need to change to support your goals.

Remember the affirmations: "I am worthy of unconditional love"; "My self worth is independent of others' opinions"; "I love and approve of myself and am at peace with my own feelings"; "I forgive myself and others, release the past and move forward with love in my heart"; "I open my heart to unconditional love for myself and others"; "I easily cut through the cords that bind me".

While your body, mind and spirit integrate those positive aspects of being and becoming more in line with your goals, become aware again of your root chakra 1 at the base of the spine allowing yourself to be secure in your decision to change; moving up to chakra 2 at the navel, feel the joy of establishing a new relationship with you – one of health and well-being. As you become aware of chakra 3 at the solar plexus you might be able to feel the control of being in charge of your life especially as it relates to Gaining Lightness. At chakra 4 at the heart, you may feel a sense of unconditional love for yourself, letting go of any negative thought patterns that up until now have held you back from your goals.

As you move up to chakra 5 at the throat, you may feel a revitalized sense of expression, one that allows you to speak your mind tactfully when others, intentionally or not, try to steer you from your path. In chakra 6, using the concept of a third eye, it might be easy for you now to create a vision of your ideal self, at your ideal weight and level of health. (Pause) As you become aware of the crown chakra at the top of your head, you can reconnect to all that is you. This is your connection with the field of all possibilities. Recognize that your goals will be achieved successfully as you connect with this divine energy and accept your role as a divine being. Ask, and it is given.

Celebrate your divinity as you begin to bring your awareness back into the room. Notice how it feels to be sitting or lying where you are; notice as sounds around you drift into your awareness; notice the light in the room through your eyelids; just enough light to allow you to see how easy it is to make all the changes you want to make now. Begin to move fingers and toes. When you see the number seven representing the crown chakra appear in your mind's eye in the next fifteen or twenty seconds, you can just drift off to sleep, not paying any attention to the rest of this session; or, if you need to be awake, you will come back fully alert, fully refreshed and fully energized.

SESSION 6:
THROAT CHAKRA MEDITATION/INDUCTION

Find a comfortable position, either sitting or lying down, and when you are ready take a few deep abdominal breaths, engaging your diaphragm muscle between your chest and abdominal cavities. Now begin to focus on your breathing. Notice when you're breathing in; notice when you're breathing out. (Pause) Wherever you are, you may hear a variety of sounds like voices, traffic, air conditioning units or other sounds. Let any outside noises be a reminder to return to focusing on your breath. Breathe in (Pause) and let it go. The conscious mind likes to think — that's what it does. So allow thoughts to drift in, float through, and drift out, letting them be a reminder to come back to your breathing. Notice when you're breathing in; notice when you're breathing out. Just let your conscious mind relax while your subconscious mind is surprised and delighted with the stories or metaphors you are about to hear. As your mind begins to relax, close your eyes and notice how it feels to just be.

Then, notice how it feels to be sitting or lying where you are. Which parts of your body are touching the chair, bed or floor; and which parts are not? Does that place where you're sitting or lying feel soft, or hard? What does the air feel like around your body? Is it warm or cool? What sounds do you hear? Consider just how relaxing those sounds can be. Then, notice the light in the room through your eyelids; just enough light to allow you to see how easy it will be to make

all the changes you want to make now.

As you return to focusing on your breath, feeling the breath going deeper and deeper into your body, become aware of your head and face. Allow those muscles to relax; and relax even more with each exhalation. (Pause) Bring your awareness to your neck and shoulders. With each breath, imagine your breath, the universal life force energy, flowing from your neck, across your shoulders, down through your arms, through your hands, and out of your body. Relaxing; releasing all tension. (Pause) Breathe into your chest and upper back, relaxing all those muscles. Then imagine breathing into your abdominal area and mid to low back. As you inhale, allow your abdomen to expand. As you breathe out, exhale fully tightening the abdominal muscles. It's like trying to make your navel touch your spine. (Pause) Imagine breathing the energy into your hips and allowing the energy to flow down through your legs, through your feet and out of your body. Relaxing; releasing all tension.

As your body becomes even more relaxed with each breath, begin to focus on your energy centers. First, at chakra number seven, at the top of your head. You may see the energy as color – seeing violet as the energy swirls. (Pause) Let the energy flow to six between the eyebrows. You don't even have to think of the color indigo here to feel the effect. (Pause) Bring the energy, your breath down to five at the throat; allowing the color blue to fill this space; noticing your body relaxing even more. (Pause) Let the energy flow to four at your heart center. Be filled with the color green as you relax even deeper. With each breath, you can go deeper and deeper into relaxation; going just to the right level of relaxation to make all the changes you want to make. (Pause) And, the breath goes even deeper to three at your solar

plexus. As you think of the color yellow, allow your body to let go and just be. (Pause) You can let that swirling energy flow all the way down to two, at your navel; let the color orange calm your abdominal area. Relaxing; releasing all tension. (Pause) Now, allow your breath to flow through your head, neck, chest, and abdomen and go all the way down to one, at the base of your spine where you may imagine the color red relaxing that area of your body. (Pause)

As your body relaxes, so does your mind. When your conscious mind is relaxed, you access the subconscious mind that holds the wisdom and resources to make all the changes you want to make. In this state, you can look at all aspects of your life objectively, without judgment, and begin to release any bondage you may have had to any actions, thoughts or emotions that are not in alignment with your goals. Just be with these calming, relaxing feelings for a moment or so. (Pause) Your body, mind and spirit are calm, relaxed and ready to be aware of those things that may be distracting you from perfect health and wellness. And ready to become aware of those things that will move you toward your goal.

As you allow each breath to take you deeper and deeper into relaxation, imagine you are walking on a path in a quiet, serene place. It might be a meadow with beautiful flowers and plants; or it might be a wooded area with a babbling brook nearby. Notice the colors, bright vibrant colors; relaxing colors; all the colors of the rainbow that occur in abundance in nature. Then, listen to the sounds of nature as you are walking along. There might be birds chirping or crickets making that little sound they make; they all seem so calming, so peaceful as your mind relaxes even more. Become aware of any fragrances associated with that place;

pleasant fragrances. Breathe them in; breathe them out. You find them mesmerizing as they allow you to relax even more deeply. Notice the peaceful, relaxing feelings you can experience – now; in this beautiful environment.

While you are on this path; the right path, you can notice an archway ahead, covered in ivy. Through the opening there appears to be a magical garden, a place of enchantment. It's kind of unusual because everything in the garden is a shade of blue; much like the energy of the throat chakra. The variety of shades of blue is very relaxing and calming. Just before you enter, take a slow deep breath and as you step into the magical garden exhale as it causes you to relax even more. Then, you notice that before you, sitting on a huge light blue mushroom in the center of the garden is a big blue frog – it's a beautiful cobalt blue. It is a sight you may have never seen before and it intrigues you. As you gain the courage you need to approach the big blue frog you notice it smiling—almost as if it has something important to say to you. The frog invites you to sit on a mushroom next to it and while you're focusing on your throat chakra, it begins to tell you telepathically of its metamorphosis from tadpole to frog.

The big blue frog tells you of its beginning as a tadpole, stuck in a pool of water, seeming to have no way out; swimming aimlessly; relying only on the advice of other creatures stuck in the pool. You too may have felt at times that you were stuck, having difficulty speaking out; feeling like you can't be heard; unable to speak your truth; feeling like you're invisible because no one pays attention to what you say and unfortunately making yourself very visible by expanding your physical form. Others who are also stuck in your pool may have given you lip service about you needing to change, but providing no useful tools to help you do it. You may have found their words hard to swallow; actually seeing these people as a pain in the neck. Or, you may have found it difficult to say no when you were tempted to eat things that were not in alignment with your goals; or perhaps you found yourself biting off more than you could chew; feeling stuffed and lethargic.

But the tadpole gives us hope because as the tadpole seeks out a new direction it begins to transform. Magically, it changes its shape and its size just as easily as it is for you to change your shape and your size as you transform into that ideal you. Once the metamorphosis happens, the newly emerged frog is able to climb out of that pool, releasing the stuckness it once experienced; and now, like you, has more options and can make different choices. It makes you think of eating smaller quantities of food; adding more fruits and vegetables to your diet; drinking more water to maintain fullness without adding calories; and exercising daily to burn off any excess calories.

The big blue frog tells you that the letters forming its name really mean Forgiving Really Old Guilt. The transformation allows you to let go of negative thought patterns giving you the ability to be who you really are; recognizing that who you really are is not one who totally fills your energy aura with physical form—leaving you room to breathe deeply and to expand your awareness about all the options you have for Gaining Lightness. You find it easy to speak your truth. And, you'll know when to accept others' words as truth— when their words actively support your goals.

The big blue frog tells you that the letters forming its name can also mean Finally Relying On Genuineness. As you become the newly transformed you, self expression becomes easier; you find it easy to respect your goals; you can assertively turn down extra food without the guilt of hurting another's feelings because it's now easy to speak your truth. You will easily see your ideal self when trying to decide whether or not to eat something that isn't in alignment with your goals. If you choose to eat it, you can do it without guilt because you will eat it in smaller quantities, consciously consuming it so that your body registers fullness before you take in too much.

Again, visualize the big blue frog with that great big smile. It's happy that you are understanding the message of transformation; understanding that change happens easily if you let it; understanding that the change is freeing; opening you to new options that support your goals. The big blue frog is happy that you are finding your smile and experiencing the joy of metamorphosis, transformation and change. Just let it happen.

The big blue frog shares more of its wisdom with you because it understands the function of the thyroid gland located in the area of the throat chakra. The frog reminds you of the importance of the thyroid gland in controlling metabolism – your body's amazing ability to transform food into energy. As you bring your awareness to the throat, you can imagine resetting the efficiency level of the thyroid gland making it easier for your body to process the foods you consume. But the big blue frog is quite the telepathic story teller and loves a good metaphor.

Take in the wisdom of the frog as it explains that the thyroid gland is shaped somewhat like a butterfly and like the frog being transformed from a tadpole, the butterfly is transformed from a caterpillar. Caterpillars are stuck in a form that is restricting and not liking themselves very much, so they enjoy engaging in the process of metamorphosis.

When the caterpillar has the irresistible urge to change, it creates a cocoon, much like going into meditation, and while inside during the transformation, the caterpillar becomes nothing more than a yellow, gooey, sticky mess, that resembles excess fat; but emerges a more beautiful thing; light and free; no longer restricted. When you have the irresistible urge to change, like now, you can go into that cocoon of introspection. Sometimes the turmoil created seems like that yellow, gooey, sticky mess but with perseverance, you will emerge transformed. Unlike the caterpillar in the cocoon feeling imprisoned by its environment, you have the freedom to be engaged and involved in the process of change.

From tadpole to frog; from caterpillar to butterfly; from your current physical condition, shape, size and emotional state to the ideal you; nature is full of transformations. Who knew that a big blue frog would be so full of wisdom? As you get up from the mushroom where you are sitting, thank the big blue frog and continue on your path to Gaining Lightness. Imagine leaving the magical garden; a place of enchantment and again notice ALL the colors of nature: the reds, the oranges, the yellows, the greens, the blues, the indigos, and the violets; the full spectrum of living color.

As the path leads you back to your current surroundings, accept the power of your mind and remember the affirmations you can express through the throat chakra: "I speak my truth"; "I communicate with my inner self to determine how much to eat"; "My body is an expression of my inner beauty"; "I maintain a healthy body image each and every step along my path to Gaining Lightness"; "I allow my higher self to speak through me".

While your body, mind and spirit integrate those positive aspects of being and becoming more in line with your goals, become aware again of your root chakra 1 at the base of the spine allowing yourself to be secure in your decision to change; moving up to chakra 2 at the navel, feel the joy of establishing a new relationship with you – one of health and well-being. As you become aware of chakra 3 at the solar plexus you might be able to feel the control of being in charge of your life especially as it relates to Gaining Lightness. At chakra 4 at the heart, you may feel a sense of unconditional love for yourself, letting go of any negative thought patterns that up until now have held you back from your goals.

As you move up to chakra 5 at the throat, you may feel a revitalized sense of expression, one that allows you to speak your mind tactfully when others, intentionally or not, try to steer you from your path. In chakra 6, using the concept of a third eye, it might be easy for you now to create a vision of your ideal self, at your ideal weight and level of health. (Pause) As you become aware of the crown chakra at the top of your head, you can reconnect to all that is you. This is your connection with the field of all possibilities. Recognize that your goals will be achieved successfully as you connect with this divine energy and accept your role as a divine being. Ask, and it is given.

Celebrate your divinity as you begin to bring your awareness back into the room. Notice how it feels to be sitting or lying where you are; notice as sounds around you drift into your awareness; notice the light in the room through your eyelids; just enough light to allow you to see how easy it is to make all the changes you want to make now. Begin to move fingers and toes. When you see the number seven representing the crown chakra appear in your mind's eye in the next fifteen or twenty seconds, you can just drift off to sleep, not paying any attention to the rest of this session; or, if you need to be awake, you will come back fully alert, fully refreshed and fully energized.

SESSION 7:

THIRD EYE CHAKRA MEDITATION/INDUCTION

Find a comfortable position, either sitting or lying down, and when you are ready take a few deep abdominal breaths, engaging your diaphragm muscle between your chest and abdominal cavities. Now begin to focus on your breathing. Notice when you're breathing in; notice when you're breathing out. (Pause) Wherever you are, you may hear a variety of sounds like voices, traffic, air conditioning units or other sounds. Let any outside noises be a reminder to return to focusing on your breath. Breathe in (Pause) and let it go. The conscious mind likes to think — that's what it does. So allow thoughts to drift in, float through, and drift out, letting them be a reminder to come back to your breathing. Notice when you're breathing in; notice when you're breathing out. Just let your conscious mind relax while your subconscious mind is surprised and delighted with the stories or metaphors you are about to hear. As your mind begins to relax, close your eyes and notice how it feels to just be.

Then, notice how it feels to be sitting or lying where you are. Which parts of your body are touching the chair, bed or floor; and which parts are not? Does that place where you're sitting or lying feel soft, or hard? What does the air feel like around your body? Is it warm or cool? What sounds do you hear? Consider just how relaxing those sounds can be. Then, notice the light in the room through your eyelids; just enough light to allow you to see how easy it will be to make

all the changes you want to make now.

As you return to focusing on your breath, feeling the breath going deeper and deeper into your body, become aware of your head and face. Allow those muscles to relax; and relax even more with each exhalation. (Pause) Bring your awareness to your neck and shoulders. With each breath, imagine your breath, the universal life force energy, flowing from your neck, across your shoulders, down through your arms, through your hands, and out of your body. Relaxing; releasing all tension. (Pause) Breathe into your chest and upper back, relaxing all those muscles. Then imagine breathing into your abdominal area and mid to low back. As you inhale, allow your abdomen to expand. As you breathe out, exhale fully tightening the abdominal muscles. It's like trying to make your navel touch your spine. (Pause) Imagine breathing the energy into your hips and allowing the energy to flow down through your legs, through your feet and out of your body. Relaxing; releasing all tension.

As your body becomes even more relaxed with each breath, begin to focus on your energy centers. First, at chakra number seven, at the top of your head. You may see the energy as color – seeing violet as the energy swirls. (Pause) Let the energy flow to six between the eyebrows. You don't even have to think of the color indigo here to feel the effect. (Pause) Bring the energy, your breath down to five at the throat; allowing the color blue to fill this space; noticing your body relaxing even more. (Pause) Let the energy flow to four at your heart center. Be filled with the color green as you relax even deeper. With each breath, you can go deeper and deeper into relaxation; going just to the right level of relaxation to make all the changes you want to make. (Pause) And, the breath goes even deeper to three at your solar

plexus. As you think of the color yellow, allow your body to let go and just be. (Pause) You can let that swirling energy flow all the way down to two, at your navel; let the color orange calm your abdominal area. Relaxing; releasing all tension. (Pause) Now, allow your breath to flow through your head, neck, chest, and abdomen and go all the way down to one, at the base of your spine where you may imagine the color red relaxing that area of your body. (Pause)

As your body relaxes, so does your mind. When your conscious mind is relaxed, you access the subconscious mind that holds the wisdom and resources to make all the changes you want to make. In this state, you can look at all aspects of your life objectively, without judgment, and begin to release any bondage you may have had to any actions, thoughts or emotions that are not in alignment with your goals. Just be with these calming, relaxing feelings for a moment or so. (Pause) Your body, mind and spirit are calm, relaxed and ready to be aware of those things that may be distracting you from perfect health and wellness. And ready to become aware of those things that will move you toward your goal.

The sixth chakra is the third eye. You've already experienced the first and second eyes. The first eye is one that looks outward toward those basic needs of safety, security. It is the "I" that realizes that I am alive and worthy of all that is good in my life; I am in control of my choices. You know that eating foods in moderate quantities will give you more safety and security with your health. You know that you'll feel better and look better, easily attaining your goals; easily attaining success with your new eating habits.

As you continue on your path to Gaining Lightness, you may have noticed how your relationships change to meet your needs; to meet your goals; to achieve success. Your relationship with food becomes one in which you gain satisfaction in making healthy choices: eating smaller portions; enjoying moderation; chewing your food more slowly while eating consciously; waiting until one bite is thoroughly chewed and swallowed before taking the next bite; finding it easy to say no to seconds and heavy desserts.

You know that keeping your goal and ideal image in mind at meals and social gatherings keeps you in control of what you eat and how consciously you eat it. Noticing that you are making the right choices in your food selections and controlling the amount of food you consume - always in moderation. Remembering that at any time, you can go back to your inner control room and reset the switches to be in alignment with your goals.

The second eye is the "I" that says that I am worthy of love and I am worthy of the ability to express myself in this existence. In your heart chakra you have looked inward to be able to accept all the love that you deserve. You continually love yourself more and more as you enjoy your success in achieving a more healthful lifestyle; a lifestyle that gives you more choices; one that gives you more energy and vitality; a lifestyle that not only adds years to your life, but also adds life to your years. With your heart chakra, you have also projected love outward to those who love you and support you in your goals; those who share in your joy of success on your path to Gaining Lightness.

You have experienced the outward expression of your desires to regain and maintain a healthy lifestyle. You've expressed the affirmations that keep you focused on your progress and success. You let the throat be the gatekeeper to the digestive system, expressing to you when enough has passed by; and expressing to you when it's time to stop eating.

Bring your awareness again to the third eye; that place right between the eyebrows. This is the "I" that means if I can imagine it, I can manifest it in my life. It's the I that can take those inner desires of safety and security; creating healthy relationships with people and food; gaining self control; giving and receiving love; being able to express yourself assertively; and project outwardly the image of your ideal self into the immediate and distant future. This is a future of feeling better, looking better and achieving your personal best.

And now as you hear the numbers from 5 to 1, allow yourself to go deeper inside; feeling more deeply relaxed. 5 - Breathing in confidence; assertiveness. 4 - Breathing in the love that you so much deserve; the love that will keep you focused on your goals; the love of your new healthy self. 3 - Breathing in personal power, self control; the control that reminds you to always eat in moderation; the control that reminds you that it's ok to just say no; the control that motivates you to exercise your body regularly. 2 - Breathing in the qualities of a new relationship with yourself; a new relationship with food; eating only when you're hungry; eating small quantities and chewing the food slowly and consciously to enjoy the flavors; stopping when you feel full. 1 - Breathing in the security of the new healthy you; breathing in the security of being comfortable with a smaller body; breathing in the security that you make the right decisions on what and how much to eat; and how much exercise is just right for you.

As you breathe deeply and allow your body and mind to go deeper into relaxation, focus on your third eye, that place where if you can imagine it, you can make it happen in your life. Imagine yourself going into a movie theater. The lighting is perfect for relaxation and this is a personal showing just for you. Imagine the theater has stadium seating and you are standing at the top. There are stairs leading down to each row and you begin to walk down them to get you to the perfect seat, which is just 5 steps away; each step taking you deeper inside. Stepping from 5 to 4, you begin to wonder what this picture is all about. Stepping down to 3 you prepare to go deep inside - the theater. Stepping down to 2, you let go of all preconceived notions of what to expect. At step 1, you find the perfect seat. Imagine yourself sitting down, and as you do, you find that the seat is comfortable and relaxing. It feels good to be there. As you look forward with your mind's eye, picture a big white screen in front of you.

As you're watching the blank screen, the title of the picture appears as "Gaining Weight". Start the movie back as far in your life as necessary to begin to see when it was that you began to behave in a way that contributed to your gaining weight. What were the situations? (Pause) What foods were involved? They were probably heavy foods that made you feel sluggish and uncomfortable. (Pause) Who are the people involved? (Pause) How did you feel about yourself? (Pause) What emotions were you experiencing? (Pause) What emotions or situations caused you to overeat? (Pause) How did you feel about the way you looked and felt? (Pause)

Now as you watch the screen, there is a scene interrupt – it says: This program has been discontinued! Inner research shows that these scenarios are no longer in your reality. And a new title appears on the screen. The new title is "You, Gaining Lightness". Imagine yourself in a situation that would involve you eating a meal. What you see now is you eating healthful foods; eating smaller portions; using smaller plates; chewing your food well to enjoy the taste and to help your metabolism work more efficiently; being able to assertively refuse food you don't need or want. See yourself in social situations eating small amounts of food to be sociable, but eating in moderation. See yourself enjoying conversations with others as you avoid the food table. (Pause) As you watch the picture of You, Gaining Lightness, you see yourself drinking water before every meal to help you feel full quicker and to set the conditions for efficient metabolism of the foods you do eat.

Continuing to watch the movie screen, as the scenes progress, the caption says "The new you". In this scene it is easy for you to see the image of you at your ideal weight. Notice the clothes you're wearing; notice the trim, fit body you now have. Imagine how you'll feel in a variety of social situations, always making the right food choices; notice how it feels to have met your goals and achieved success. Imagine those things you may be able to do now because you feel better and have more energy. You've found some sort of exercise activity that you enjoy and do regularly. You enjoy eating in moderation. You may even be able to imagine someone joining you in this scene; someone who loves and supports you. What would this person who loves you and supports you say to you, knowing you've honored your commitment to yourself, achieved your goals and were successful in Gaining Lightness? (Pause) And, notice how that makes you feel; a perfect ending to the movie about the new you.

As you get ready to leave the theater feeling good about yourself and all that you've accomplished, in your mind's eye, begin to go back up the steps. One, knowing you already know how to be your ideal weight. Two, feeling confident that your subconscious mind holds the resources you need to reach your ideal weight. Three, feeling successful with the changes you've already made. Four, ready to become what you can truly be - successful. Five, trusting your body's wisdom to guide you in making all the right food choices.

Letting go of the image of the theater, bring your awareness to the place where you are now and remember that what you focus your attention on will manifest in your life! What you believe determines how you behave. How you behave determines what you become. What you become determines what your world will become.

Accept the new beliefs found in these affirmations: "I easily release unwanted beliefs that no longer serve my purpose"; "I continually progress toward my ideal body image"; "I accept my inner power and resources to effect continual change"; "I joyfully release all self doubt and choose a positive way of thinking"; "I believe in my heart that with focused intention I easily attain and maintain my ideal weight".

While your body, mind and spirit integrate those positive aspects of being and becoming more in line with your goals, become aware again of your root chakra 1 at the base of the spine allowing yourself to be secure in your decision to change; moving up to chakra 2 at the navel, feel the joy of establishing a new relationship with you – one of health and well-being. As you become aware of chakra 3 at the solar plexus you might be able to feel the control of being in charge of your life especially as it relates to Gaining Lightness. At chakra 4 at the heart, you may feel a sense of unconditional love for yourself, letting go of any negative

thought patterns that up until now have held you back from your goals.

As you move up to chakra 5 at the throat, you may feel a revitalized sense of expression, one that allows you to speak your mind tactfully when others, intentionally or not, try to steer you from your path. In chakra 6, using the concept of a third eye, it might be easy for you now to create a vision of your ideal self, at your ideal weight and level of health. (Pause) As you become aware of the crown chakra at the top of your head, you can reconnect to all that is you. This is your connection with the field of all possibilities. Recognize that your goals will be achieved successfully as you connect with this divine energy and accept your role as a divine being. Ask, and it is given.

Celebrate your divinity as you begin to bring your awareness back into the room. Notice how it feels to be sitting or lying where you are; notice as sounds around you drift into your awareness; notice the light in the room through your eyelids; just enough light to allow you to see how easy it is to make all the changes you want to make now. Begin to move fingers and toes. When you see the number seven representing the crown chakra appear in your mind's eye in the next fifteen or twenty seconds, you can just drift off to sleep, not paying any attention to the rest of this session; or, if you need to be awake, you will come back fully alert, fully refreshed and fully energized.

SESSION 8:

CROWN CHAKRA MEDITATION/INDUCTION

Find a comfortable position, either sitting or lying down, and when you are ready take a few deep abdominal breaths, engaging your diaphragm muscle between your chest and abdominal cavities. Now begin to focus on your breathing. Notice when you're breathing in; notice when you're breathing out. (Pause) Wherever you are, you may hear a variety of sounds like voices, traffic, air conditioning units or other sounds. Let any outside noises be a reminder to return to focusing on your breath. Breathe in (Pause) and let it go. The conscious mind likes to think — that's what it does. So allow thoughts to drift in, float through, and drift out, letting them be a reminder to come back to your breathing. Notice when you're breathing in; notice when you're breathing out. Just let your conscious mind relax while your subconscious mind is surprised and delighted with the stories or metaphors you are about to hear. As your mind begins to relax, close your eyes and notice how it feels to just be.

Then, notice how it feels to be sitting or lying where you are. Which parts of your body are touching the chair, bed or floor; and which parts are not? Does that place where you're sitting or lying feel soft, or hard? What does the air feel like around your body? Is it warm or cool? What sounds do you hear? Consider just how relaxing those sounds can be. Then, notice the light in the room through your eyelids; just enough light to allow you to see how easy it will be to make

all the changes you want to make now.

As you return to focusing on your breath, feeling the breath going deeper and deeper into your body, become aware of your head and face. Allow those muscles to relax; and relax even more with each exhalation. (Pause) Bring your awareness to your neck and shoulders. With each breath, imagine your breath, the universal life force energy, flowing from your neck, across your shoulders, down through your arms, through your hands, and out of your body. Relaxing; releasing all tension. (Pause) Breathe into your chest and upper back, relaxing all those muscles. Then imagine breathing into your abdominal area and mid to low back. As you inhale, allow your abdomen to expand. As you breathe out, exhale fully tightening the abdominal muscles. It's like trying to make your navel touch your spine. (Pause) Imagine breathing the energy into your hips and allowing the energy to flow down through your legs, through your feet and out of your body. Relaxing; releasing all tension.

As your body becomes even more relaxed with each breath, begin to focus on your energy centers. First, at chakra number seven, at the top of your head. You may see the energy as color – seeing violet as the energy swirls. (Pause) Let the energy flow to six between the eyebrows. You don't even have to think of the color indigo here to feel the effect. (Pause) Bring the energy, your breath down to five at the throat; allowing the color blue to fill this space; noticing your body relaxing even more. (Pause) Let the energy flow to four at your heart center. Be filled with the color green as you relax even deeper. With each breath, you can go deeper and deeper into relaxation; going just to the right level of relaxation to make all the changes you want to make. (Pause) And, the breath goes even deeper to three at your solar

plexus. As you think of the color yellow, allow your body to let go and just be. (Pause) You can let that swirling energy flow all the way down to two, at your navel; let the color orange calm your abdominal area. Relaxing; releasing all tension. (Pause) Now, allow your breath to flow through your head, neck, chest, and abdomen and go all the way down to one, at the base of your spine where you may imagine the color red relaxing that area of your body. (Pause)

As your body relaxes, so does your mind. When your conscious mind is relaxed, you access the subconscious mind that holds the wisdom and resources to make all the changes you want to make. In this state, you can look at all aspects of your life objectively, without judgment, and begin to release any bondage you may have had to any actions, thoughts or emotions that are not in alignment with your goals. Just be with these calming, relaxing feelings for a moment or so. (Pause) Your body, mind and spirit are calm, relaxed and ready to be aware of those things that may be distracting you from perfect health and wellness. And ready to become aware of those things that will move you toward your goal.

Your subconscious mind is the storehouse of all your memories, skills and resources, so your subconscious mind knows more than your conscious mind does; and if your subconscious mind knows more than your conscious mind does, then you really know more than you think you do. As you focus on the crown chakra at the top of your head, know that this is the energy center that has direct contact with divine spirit. And, because you know there is a connection it is due to your faith, faith that there is a divine entity; one that is all powerful; one that is so powerful that it has created and guides the functioning of the entire universe - the external universe as well as your internal universe. Only you know if you do have the faith in yourself to surrender to this divine intelligence and accept all that you deserve. Wouldn't it be interesting to meet this divine spirit and tap into that infinite wisdom?

You may have heard it said, or seen it written that the kingdom of this spirit lies within you. Allow each breath to take you deeper inside; deeper into relaxation; deeper into the field of all possibilities that is accessed through your crown chakra. As you experience this within-ness, you know that it is with thin-ness that you achieve your goals. Breathing in inspiration; and as you're breathing out letting go; opening to the possibilities; anticipating being filled; and fulfilled; with possibilities; endless and inspiring. As you do, remember that you already possess the attributes that you seek most passionately. You already hold all the power you need to make any change you are passionate about making.

Amazingly, there is a place on your head that you call your temple. As you focus on that area, going deep within, imagine what that temple might look like. It might be a large stone structure with ivy growing on the sides, and beautiful stained glass windows; or it may be a more humble place, but still a place of inspiration. Becoming aware again of your breathing; your inspiration; imagine what it might be like to go within the temple. As you create the image, see yourself standing outside the temple knowing that all the motivation you need to continue Gaining Lightness lies within. Feel yourself pulsating with anticipation; pulsating with the anticipation of connecting with that divine spirit that is continually in direct contact with your subconscious mind; directing the functions of all your body systems without your awareness; becoming aware that this divine energy is always encouraging you to go in the right direction; staying on the path; the right path; the path to Gaining Lightness.

In your mind's eye, see yourself walking up to the door. And, as you open the door, feeling yourself opening to spiritual guidance, you see the inside of the temple. It's illuminated with lightness. You might see this light as white with a hint of a violet hue; inside you. It's calming; relaxing; inviting. Notice what things or symbols are around the temple; supporting your comfort, allowing you to feel safe and relaxed. You may sense the fragrance of incense or flowers. And, you may be able to feel the presence of God, or the Goddess; the divine spirit that resides in you; inspiring you; guiding you. It is a holy place, where you can experience the holiness; the wholeness of you; and be wholly filled with inspiration; breathing in love, joy, peace and confidence; breathing out fear, anxiety and all negativity. In this temple you feel warm, relaxed, peaceful, weightless. Becoming lighter and lighter; Gaining Lightness; connecting with your self on new levels. Finding inner awareness of who and what you truly are. Let go of restraints and just be.

Now, deep inside the temple, find a place with your mind's eye where you can sit comfortably. And then, allow the image representing your conceptualization of the God, the Goddess, the divine spirit to appear before you. This being always loves you and supports you and wants you to have everything you desire — ask and you shall receive. You can ask this spirit what the root cause of your previous weight gain was; and listen for the answer. (Pause) You can ask this spirit to free you from all the reasons you let this happen. With the success you are experiencing now, you know that through divine spirit, all things are possible; the possibility of you feeling healthy; comfortable; easily attaining and maintaining your ideal weight. As you become free from the bondage of any past restraints, ask the entity for the inspiration; the confidence; the pleasure of staying on the path to Gaining Lightness; guiding you and assisting you with healthy food choices; giving you the control over all temptation; motivating you to exercise your body regularly; keeping you always focused on your goals — making the right choices; the light choices; relying on the lightness within to illuminate your path.

You can ask the divine spirit to always be with you, making all of your outward actions and choices as easy and effortless as the inner actions that are automatic, like breathing, your inspiration; the beating of your heart; reminding you of the love of divine spirit; and your metabolism, transforming all that you ingest to support your health and well being; eliminating all that does not support your goals. As you breathe in the inspiration of spirit, quiet your body and mind and feel all the internal workings of your body. Notice how it just happens without you having to exert any effort. Just as your subconscious mind, in harmony with spirit guides all these internal actions effortlessly, your subconscious mind in harmony with spirit can guide all your external actions effortlessly. In fact, each breath you take inspires you to make all the right food choices and exercise your body consistently to attain and maintain your ideal weight.

Then, looking around the inside of the temple, notice if there is a symbol that seems significant to you and will remind you, once you leave the temple, of your goals every time you see the symbol. If nothing seems to resonate with you now, just touch together the tips of your thumb and index finger on your dominant hand, a symbol that means

OK. Whichever symbol you choose, from this moment forward, use that symbol to remind you of your goals each time you are faced with a choice: to eat more, or less; to loaf, or exercise. As you fully anchor your symbol, thank divine spirit for being there for you and supporting you. Imagine then getting up and leaving the temple, remembering you can always return there for inspiration and direction. You feel secure knowing that you have joined with the unified field of consciousness to gain the love and support you need to meet your goals. Let the path lead you back to the temple area on your head feeling the warmth, the calmness, the inspiration, the satisfaction of success. Right here, right now.

As you fill your awareness with the power of the seventh chakra, you can use the following affirmations to continue on your path to Gaining Lightness: "I willingly accept the divine guidance of the universe"; "I continually access the unified field of consciousness to attain my goals"; "I am open to divine intervention on my path to Gaining Lightness"; "I open myself to the miracles from the power of the universal life force energy"; "I continually expand my power of imagination to be the change I seek".

While your body, mind and spirit integrate those positive aspects of being and becoming more in line with your goals, become aware again of your root chakra 1 at the base of the spine allowing yourself to be secure in your decision to change; moving up to chakra 2 at the navel, feel the joy of establishing a new relationship with you – one of health and well-being. As you become aware of chakra 3 at the solar plexus you might be able to feel the control of being in charge of your life especially as it relates to Gaining Lightness. At chakra 4 at the heart, you may feel a sense of unconditional love for yourself, letting go of any negative

thought patterns that up until now have held you back from your goals.

As you move up to chakra 5 at the throat, you may feel a revitalized sense of expression, one that allows you to speak your mind tactfully when others, intentionally or not, try to steer you from your path. In chakra 6, using the concept of a third eye, it might be easy for you now to create a vision of your ideal self, at your ideal weight and level of health. (Pause) As you become aware of the crown chakra at the top of your head, you can reconnect to all that is you. This is your connection with the field of all possibilities. Recognize that your goals will be achieved successfully as you connect with this divine energy and accept your role as a divine being. Ask, and it is given.

Celebrate your divinity as you begin to bring your awareness back into the room. Notice how it feels to be sitting or lying where you are; notice as sounds around you drift into your awareness; notice the light in the room through your eyelids; just enough light to allow you to see how easy it is to make all the changes you want to make now. Begin to move fingers and toes. When you see the number seven representing the crown chakra appear in your mind's eye in the next fifteen or twenty seconds, you can just drift off to sleep, not paying any attention to the rest of this session; or, if you need to be awake, you will come back fully alert, fully refreshed and fully energized.

REFERENCES

BOOKS

Chips, Allen, DCH
Clinical Hypnotherapy: A Transpersonal Approach
EIH Publishing,
Division of the Eastern Institute of Hypnotherapy,
Goshen, VA, 1999

Green, Joey
The Zen of Oz, Ten Spiritual Lessons from
Over the Rainbow
Renaissance Books, Los Angeles, CA, 1998

Govinda, Kalashatra
A Handbook of Chakra Healing
Ullstein Heyne List GmbH & Co. 2002
Konecky & Konecky Old Saybrook, CT, 2004

Horton, William D., Psy. D.
NFNLP Basic Practitioner Workbook
National Federation of NeuroLinguistic Psychology
Venice FL, 2006

I.S.F.T.A.
The Transition from Rehab to Fitness
International Sports and Fitness Trainer's
Association, 2003

Judith, Anodea, Ph.D.
  Wheels of Life
  Llewellyn Publishing, St. Paul Minnesota
  Second Edition, 1999
Malat, Randy, M.S., Arnett, Amy K. & Freedman,
Marjorie, Ph.D., M.S.,
  Institute For Natural Resources Health Update
  February 2004

Myss, Caroline, Ph.D.
  Anatomy of the Spirit, The Seven Stages of
  Power and Healing
  Harmony Books, New York, NY 1996

Nelson, P.
  There's a Hole In My Sidewalk
  Popular Library N. Y. Mar. '77
  Box 5755 Terre Haute, IN 47805

Roizen, Michael F., M.D. and Oz, Mehmet C., M.D.
  You on a Diet, The Owner's Manual for
  Waist Management
  Free Press, New York, NY, 2006

Shoebox Book
  The Guru Guy Guide to the Meaning of Life and
  Other Mysteries of the Universe
  Hallmark Cards, Inc., 1998

Wills, Pauline
  Chakra Workbook
  Eddison Sadd Editions Limited, London, 2002

WEBSITES

nutristrategy.com

thedietchannel.com

thinkexist.com

BOB WOLFE'S WEBSITES

gaininglightness.com

reflexologystuff.com

PATSY SYKES' WEBSITE

awakeningspiritonline.com